THE
Prayer Book
REVEALED

A Brief Illustrated History of the Book of Common Prayer

Peter S. Paine

The Prayer Book Revealed

First published 2023 by Beaten Track Publishing
Copyright © 2023 Peter S. Paine

All rights reserved.

No part of this publication may be reproduced, stored in a retrieval system, or transmitted, in any form or by any means, without the prior permission of the publisher, nor be otherwise circulated without the publisher's prior consent in any form of binding or cover other than that in which it is published and without a similar condition including this condition being imposed on the subsequent publisher.

The moral right of the author has been asserted.

Paperback ISBN: 978 1 78645 602 1
eBook ISBN: 978 1 78645 603 8

Beaten Track Publishing,
Burscough, Lancashire.
www.beatentrackpublishing.com

Dedicated to my late father

The Reverend Humphrey John Paine
1906–1989

THE
Prayer Book
REVEALED

*A Brief Illustrated History of
the Book of Common Prayer*

by Peter S. Paine

Foreword by
The Rt Revd Humphrey Southern,
Bishop of Repton

CONTENTS

Foreword 1

Introduction 3

Chapter 1: Lay Worship Prior to the Reformation 5

Appendix 1 14

Chapter 2: The First Prayer Book of Edward VI, 1549 15

Chapter 3: The 1552 Revision and the Elizabethan Settlement 31

Appendix 2 43

Chapter 4: The Early Stuarts 45

Chapter 5: The 1662 Revision and Seventeenth-Century Additions 53

Appendix 3 64

Chapter 6: The Non-Jurors and The Prayer Book in the Eighteenth Century 65

Chapter 7: Scotland, America and Ireland 73

Appendix 4 80

Chapter 8: Printers, Publications and Illustrations 81

Chapter 9: Prayer Book Revision in the Nineteenth and Twentieth Centuries 97

Chapter 10: The Spirituality of the Book of Common Prayer 111

Epilogue 119

Appendix 5 123

Glossary 125

Bibliography 129

FOREWORD

Liturgical handbook, literary masterpiece, manual of devotion, historical source book, deposit of doctrine, common denominator of a disparate and divergent Christian tradition – the *Book of Common Prayer* may be characterised in many different ways. Indeed, reactions to it – of anything from awe and delight to boredom and frustration – will be significantly shaped by the expectations that are brought to it. For some, the bedrock of faith and a dependable foundation in the face of relativism and uncertainty, for others, a curious and increasingly irrelevant hangover from a distant age, it is hardly surprising that it is a little book that has commanded passionate loyalty and also attracted considerable controversy.

The Prayer Book was conceived in fertile soil, both theologically and linguistically. The sixteenth century was simultaneously a crucible of passionate theological debate and arguably the most productive era in the evolution of the English language. In not much more than a century from its original publication in 1549, it was revised and went to war over twice, proscribed twice (once for over a decade) and vilified alike by doctrinal conservatives, who deplored its innovation, and Protestant reformers, who regretted the incompleteness of the change it promised. It is easy for generations formed in the long period of stability in Church of England authorised liturgy from the second half of the seventeenth to the middle of the twentieth centuries to forget how controversial it was for so long, controversial long before the rather anaemic cultural squabbles of the eras of the so-called 1970s 'Series', the *Alternative Service Book* of 1980 and the present century's *Common Worship*. It is this story that Peter Paine offers us in this history.

Perhaps it is its timelessness, forged through the vicissitudes of its history, that is the most striking feature of the Prayer Book. Like many clergy, I have treasured the privilege of standing at the altar at the 'early service' in a country parish church turning pages carefully and respectfully defaced as sovereigns have come and gone: '... thy servant ~~VICTORIA, EDWARD, GEORGE, EDWARD, ELIZABETH~~...' and now *CHARLES*. Once – to my utter delight – I picked up in a church I was visiting a volume casually laid on a bench which fell open at the state prayers in Matins: 'Most heartily we beseech thee with thy favour to behold our most gracious Sovereign Lady, Queen *ANNE*...'

This is the book that Herbert and Donne used in the services at which they officiated, as appropriate to the rustic intimacy of Bemerton as to the grandeur of St Paul's. The Prayer Book alike of Milton, the Wesleys, Pusey and the Clapham House Set, which inspired the widely differing approaches to public worship, private devotion and theological enquiry of each of these, as of so many more. Controversial it may have been, but the lasting impression one has is of a volume loved – loved and hallowed by use through the ages and in all manner of circumstances and settings.

This present volume is a labour of love, both filial love and devotion – Peter Paine was inspired by the collection of Prayer Books amassed by his late father out of love – and love for the BCP itself. The greatest sign of love for a work such as the Prayer Book is that it should be used and enjoyed, enabled to inspire, to challenge, to reassure and to perplex the faithful, 'exciting of Piety and Devotion in the Publick Worship of God', as the 1662 Preface has it. Peter Paine here offers us a warm and inspiring resource to encourage just that enjoyment and devotion. We are in his debt.

+Humphrey Southern
St Peter's Day, 2023

INTRODUCTION

My father, the Reverend Humphrey John Paine, was brought up in a clerical family and was the grandson of the Reverend Jesse Paine. His parents, the Reverend Nigel Wood Paine and Mabel Beatrice Tylston Hodgson, moved to their Norfolk rectory in 1901. Humphrey was born there five years later; their third child and second son. It was a devotional household with one of the bedrooms in the large Victorian rectory maintained as a place of prayer. There were numerous copies of the Scriptures in their original languages. It was, however, the English *Book of Common Prayer* that was Humphrey's great interest. He began collecting copies at an early age and did so for the rest of his life, exploring the second-hand bookshops and stately homes of his native county, where books occasionally came up for sale. After curacies in the North East of England, three years in Penang before the outbreak of war, and a spell in the Royal Navy as an RNVR chaplain, he returned to Norfolk in 1945. Not only did he return to his home county but also to the very rectory in which he was born. It was there that he spent most of the rest of his ministry and made his collection of Prayer Books.

Sadly, he never wrote about them himself, but he loved to show them off and talk about them. This may be because his delight was as much in handling their fine bindings as of exploring their contents, though he was devoted to the Daily Office and a great admirer of Cranmer's Collects.

It is important to emphasise that this brief illustrated history is restricted to the contents of this Prayer Book collection of nearly one hundred volumes. It is not intended to be a comprehensive history nor an academic one. For those interested in these aspects, reference may be made to the bibliography. The collection contains copies from Elizabeth I to the present day and facsimile copies of earlier editions. The collection also includes Henry VIII's *Primer* of 1545 printed in 1710 and illustrations from a late-fifteenth-century *Book of Hours*. The story of the Prayer Book begins, therefore, before the 1549 first edition.

There is a fundamental question to be addressed before this story is told: why make a collection of the *Book of Common Prayer* and why write about it now? Of what interest is this old text to the present reader, now that the Church has moved on to a new liturgy? There will be those without any historical or liturgical interest for whom any answer will be inadequate. For those with any interest in such matters, a response may be made along these lines: the *Book of Common Prayer* of 1662 has been the authorised service book of the Church of England for three hundred years and still holds that position alongside new editions. Before that time, earlier editions were used throughout the land from 1549 with two significant interruptions when it was suppressed in the reign of Queen Mary (1553–1558) and during the Commonwealth (1649–1660). During the period of English imperial expansion, it has been used by many different peoples and translated into many languages. Its importance in the development of Anglicanism can hardly be overestimated since what we believe has been formed by the way we pray – *lex orandi, lex credendi*. At its inception in the sixteenth century, it was a compromise between conflicting opinions of doctrine and forms of worship. While some would claim this to be a weakness, J.H. Benton, writing in the early twentieth century, believed that it 'was its strength; for this made it a liturgy established by the consent and authority of the people, for the use of the people, in the common language of the people'.[i] It should be acknowledged that this 'consent' was quite fiercely protected and enforced, especially in the seventeenth century right through to the nineteenth (especially in relation to the Test Acts and non-tolerance of Roman Catholics etc.). Moreover, it was written in the finest English prose at a time when the language was at its prime in the sixteenth century by Archbishop Thomas Cranmer, one of the foremost scholars of his day.

Before the story commences, thanks are extended to Bishop Humphrey Southern, who made some helpful suggestions and corrections to the text and provided the Foreword, for which I am most grateful. Any further errors are the author's responsibility. Thanks are also extended to Debbie McGowan of Beaten Track Publishing, for her encouragement and expertise, and also to Duncan Harper for the cover design.

The worship of the medieval Church is the background to the *Book of Common Prayer*, and it is here that the story begins.

Christmas 2022

---

i Benton, 1910, p. iii.

Chapter 1

LAY WORSHIP PRIOR TO THE REFORMATION

One of Archbishop Cranmer's achievements was to reduce the number of daily services or Offices from eight to two: Matins and Evensong. The eight Offices of Matins, Lauds, Prime, Terce, Sext, None, Vespers and Compline were the pattern of Benedictine monastic prayer, though the monks often combined the first two Offices. Secular or parish clergy carried the process further. For the clergy, these eight Offices were contained in the Breviary. *The Book of Hours* and *Primer* were used by lay people.

Two developments contributed to the emergence of the *Book of Hours* and *Primers*. Pious monks added to the Offices their own private devotions: the fifteen gradual Psalms (Psalms 120–134) and the seven Penitential Psalms (Psalms 6, 32, 38, 51, 102, 130 and 143). In the thirteenth century, a revision of the Offices was popularised by the Franciscans and imposed on the churches in Europe in 1277. Saints' days and festivals displaced the normal daily Offices. The reading of Scripture was reduced and replaced with readings from the lives of the saints, which were sometimes mythical. The ordinary reading of the Psalter was broken up with increased observation of festivals and the Office of the Blessed Virgin Mary added; consequently, the Offices became more complex and increasingly the preserve of the clergy.

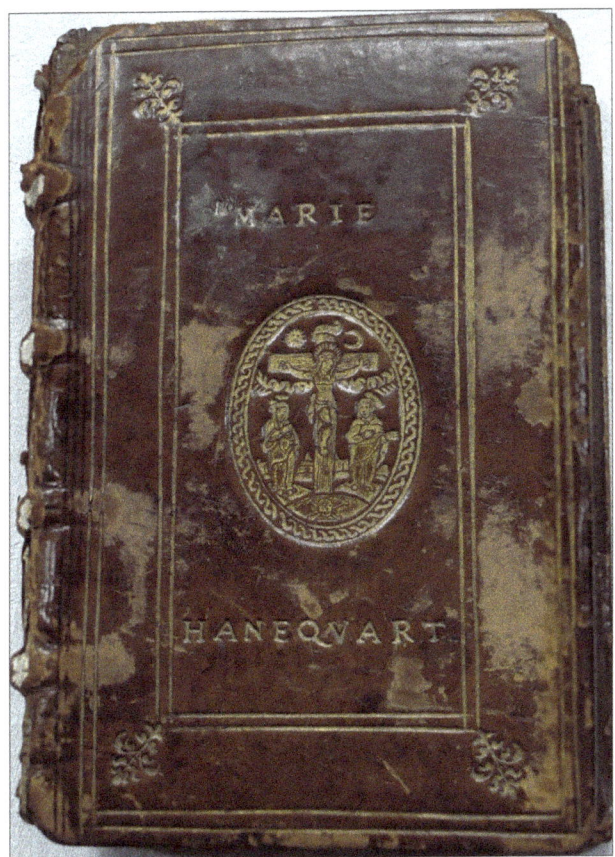

Plate 1. A 15th c. Book of Hours bound for Marie Hanequart.

The *Book of Hours* or *Primers* grew from the demands of pious laity who wished to emulate the monastic piety. There was no standard content. *The Book of Hours* illustrated here is a book of Marian devotion based around

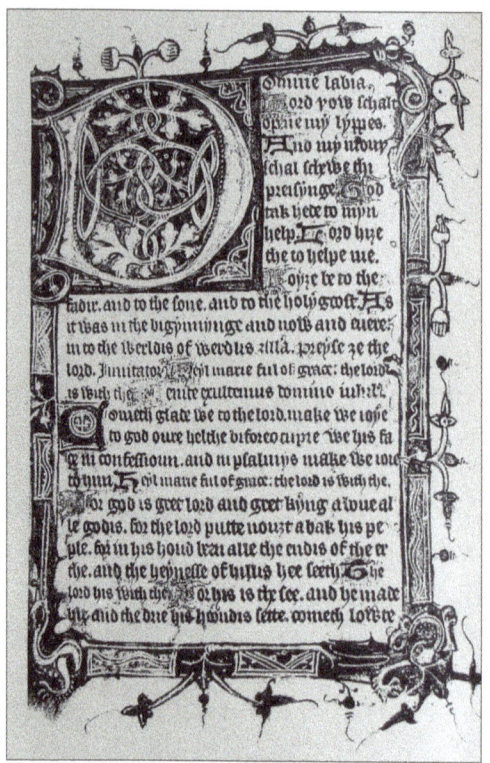

Plate 2. Facsimile 1891 of page one of the Primer or 'Prayer Book of the Lay People' of c. 1400 AD in English 'Domine labia. Lord thow schalt opene my lyppes. And my mouth schal schewe thi preisynge...' The beginning of Matins.

the Hours of the Virgin containing all eight Offices modelled on the clergy Offices but much shorter and less variable. It begins with a Calendar listing the festivals of saints throughout the year, followed by four short services: Hours of the Cross, Hours of the Holy Spirit, Mass of the Virgin Mary, Advent Offices. The Hours of the Virgin are succeeded by Penitential Psalms, Litany and Prayers, Vigil of the Dead, the Marian devotional prayer 'Obsecre te', other prayers to the Virgin and finally Prayers to Saints, of which ten are named and illustrated.

Plate 3. The Crucifixion introducing the Hours of the Cross.

Books of Hours were a very popular devotional book in the Middle Ages. It is claimed that some fifty thousand Books of Hours (or *Horae*) and *Primers* were in use by lay people in England at the end of the fifteenth century.[i] Illustrated *Horae* (see plate 1) were generally in Latin, *Primers* in the vernacular. In the last century before the Reformation, it was a book that lay people would take to Mass, read to themselves during the service and by themselves on weekdays. Their great attraction was the invariability of the services, which became as familiar to the laity as the canonical hours were to the clergy:

---

i Duffy, 2005[1992], p. 7.

[Lay people]...wanted prayers which helped them cultivate that intense relationship of affectionate, penitential intimacy with Christ and his Mother which was the lingua franca of the late Middle Ages, and they wanted prayers which focused on their day-to-day hopes and fears. They wanted books that would provide them with illustrations, indulgencies and other spiritual benefits.[ii]

Plate 4. *David at prayer with a harp introducing the Penitential Psalms.*

Two themes are outstanding. Because the Hours of the Virgin are the most significant element of the book, it could be argued that a *Book of Hours* is primarily a Marian devotional work. Besides the eight Offices, the most important Marian devotion was the prayer '*Obsecro te*' ('I implore you', holy Lady, Mother of God...), a lengthy and repetitious prayer to Mary celebrating her joys as well as her sorrows. It is nevertheless from identification with the sorrows of Mary and her grief as Christ's Mother that medieval people drew much comfort.

The visions of Julian of Norwich bearing witness to the centrality of the sufferings of Christ to medieval devotion are of primary importance in these devotional books. Christ's sufferings were a rich source of penitential reflection and the primary demonstration of his human nature and hence his credentials as Saviour of the world (plate 3). One of the invariable elements of the printed *Horae* (Hours) are the Prayers of the Passion. They were frequently based upon the wounds of Christ and his seven words from the cross. In this *Primer*, the subjects are: the sending of God's Son into the world for our salvation; the willing suffering of Christ according to the Father's will; the consecration of Christ's body and blood under the form of bread and wine; Peter's denial; the prayer of anguish of Jesus at Gethsemane; and the condemnation of the innocent Christ.

---

ii Duffy, 2005[1992], p. 234.

Each of the eight Hours of the Virgin or Little Office is preceded by an exquisite illustration (plates 6–13) related to the life of the Virgin. They demonstrated what may have been for many people the religious power of pictures over the meaning of the text. In this *Horae*, the illustration of the Coronation of the Virgin precedes the Advent Offices; the Annunciation – Matins; the Visitation to Elizabeth – Lauds; the Nativity – Prime; the Visit of the Shepherds – Terce; the Visit of the Magi – Sext; the Presentation in the Temple – None; the Massacre of the Innocents – Vespers; the Flight into Egypt – Compline. The Penitential Psalms are preceded by David at prayer with a harp (plate 4); the Vigil for the Dead by Christ at prayer with a small figure rising from his grave.

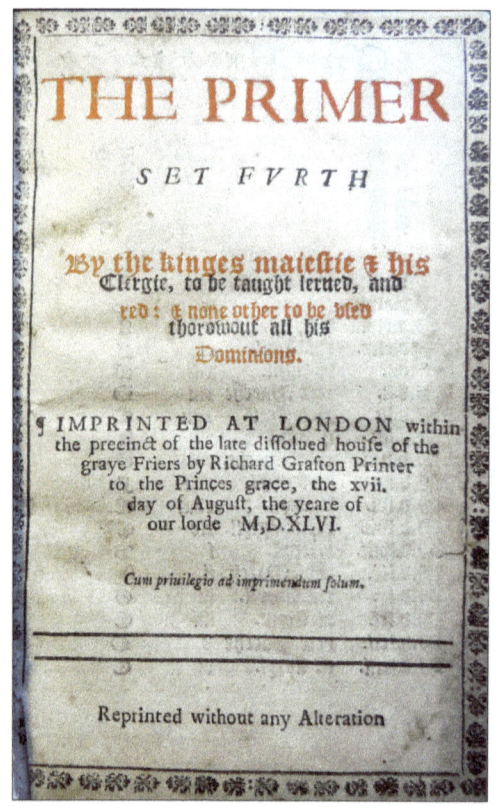

Plate 5. *King Henry's Primer of 1545 printed in 1710.*

A closer correspondence between picture and text appears with the prayers to the saints and their attributes. John the Baptist carries a lamb; SS Peter and Paul greet one another, Peter carrying keys and Paul a sword (of the Spirit); Andrew a large cross; Anthony a pig; Nicholas offering gifts to three children; Anna with Virgin and Child; Mary Magdalene an alabaster flask; Katherine a wheel; Barbara a tower; and Margaret a bear.

THE KING'S PRIMER

In 1544, Henry VIII was about to go to war with France. Attendance at the customary processional prayers for such occasions had been poor, so Henry instructed his archbishop to write a new Litany. Cranmer used the occasion to produce a vernacular version, which was to be used in procession throughout the province of Canterbury. The archbishop shortened the traditional text and drew upon other material. It was well received.

In the same year, Cranmer was under pressure from the Reformers and attempted to defuse this by issuing *The Primer, Set Forth by the King's Majestie & his Clergy*. The *King's Primer* was published, in 1545, in English. The purpose was twofold:

Plate 6. *The Annunciation introducing Matins.*

Plate 7. *The Visitation of Mary to Elizabeth – Lauds.*

Plate 8. *The Nativity introducing Prime.*

Plate 9. *The Shepherds introducing Terce.*

Plate 10. *The Magi introducing Sext.*

Plate 11. *The Presentation in the Temple – Nones.*

Plate 12. *Herod ordering the massacre of the Innocents introducing Vespers.*

Plate 13. *The flight into Egypt introducing Compline.*

'to have one uniform order of all such books throughout all our dominions'[iii] and that the people hear and so learn the Lord's Prayer, Ten Commandments and Creed in their own language (plate 5). The contents appeared to be traditional but were much changed; for instance, the number of saints' days in the Kalendar were very much reduced; the Psalms of mourning, complaint and supplication removed. The new Litany was included.

It is noteworthy that in this *Primer* written by Cranmer for King Henry, there are no prayers to the Virgin, to the Saints or most significantly to the Blessed Sacrament. Neither are there prayers for the dead, which were mocked by the Reformers: 'There is nothing in the Dirige (Vigil of the Dead) taken out of Scripture that maketh any mention of the souls departed than doth the tale of Robin Hood'.[iv] The contents of this *Primer* are compared with those of the *Primer* of c. 1400 AD in Appendix 1:

Plate 14. The Mass panel in the Seven Sacrament Font in the church of St. Mary the Virgin, Martham, Norfolk.

>These prayers point away from the lush affectivity of medieval piety, towards the starker and graver tones of Reformation. The Primer, published with all the panoply of royal approval, and with every sign of the direct involvement of the King himself, was a portent of things to come.[v]

THE LATIN MASS AND THE ORDER OF THE COMMUNION

Two of my Norfolk churches displayed architectural evidence of the medieval theology of the Latin Mass. At St Edmund's church at Thurne, there is a squint hole penetrating the four-foot-thick tower which, from the outside, stands at head height and through which there is a clear view of the altar at the other end of the building. The church of St Mary the Virgin at Martham possesses a seven-sacrament font. The Mass panel shows the back of a priest holding up a circular Host (blessed bread) which is as large as his head (plate 14).

---

iii The Primer, The King's Injunction

iv Quoted from Jacobs, 2013, p.12.

v Duffy, 2005[1992], p. 447.

These speak firstly of the central significance of the consecrated bread as the Body of Christ and secondly that *seeing* it is what was important rather than receiving it. In fact, the elevation of the Host was the only part of the Mass that the laity would have seen. The Mass had become not a communal act of worship to be shared but a moment of consecration (the sacring) to be observed, and people would run from one church to another to see as many sacrings as they could.

This practice demonstrates a profound change from a primitive understanding of the Communion as a corporate act of thanksgiving to one in which the priest acting on behalf of the Church consecrated through the words of Institution the Body and Blood of Christ. The language stressed the miraculous. It was based on the Aristotelian distinction between the 'accidents', which are seen and touched, and the 'substance', which is the ideal, abiding reality. Although the consecrated elements appear to be bread and wine, since their accidents remain, the substance, the real thing, is now the true Body and Blood of Christ. Alongside this emphasis of the presence of Christ in the elements went a parallel emphasis in Western Christendom of the sacrificial aspect of the Eucharist. The sacrifice of the Mass was, in medieval thought, the sacrifice of Calvary wherein the body and blood of Christ were offered to the Father for our sins.[vi]

Hence the elevation became the climax of the service when the laity were actually seeing their maker present among them, the Mass became a memorial of Christ's Passion, and hearing Mass had become the propitiation of a stern deity. The result was the proliferation of masses for the dead and of votive masses said to secure a particular end.

Cranmer found this deeply distressing and opposed to true Christian devotion. He wrote in his book *Defence of the True and Catholic Doctrine of the Sacrament of the Body and Blood of Christ*:

> What made the people to run from their seats to the altar, and from altar to altar, and from sacring (as they called it) to sacring at that thing which the priest held up in his hands, if they thought not to honour the thing which they saw?[vii]

The Reformed understanding of the Mass was that it was a memorial only of Christ's death 'and not a sacrifice, but a remembrance of the sacrifice that was once offered upon the cross' and 'all oblations except that of our Lord are vain and void'.[viii]

---

vi   Harrison, 1959, p. 30.

vii Referenced from Jacobs, 2013, pp. 30–31.

viii Cuming, 1969, p. 32.

With Henry VIII's death in January 1547, the reforming party were less constrained. During the previous year, a group of learned divines had assembled and agreed an 'Order of the Communion'. This comprised some (now familiar) Reformed devotions set in the Latin Roman Mass immediately after the Communion of the priest. 'The Order of the Communion' carried a proclamation by the new king, Edward VI, and began use in May 1548. The purpose of these devotions as set forth in the proclamation was to encourage every communicant to receive Communion 'with due reverence and Christian behaviour'.

Plate 15. *The Order of the Communion of 1548 title page from a facsimile edition of the Henry Bradshaw Society. London 1908.*

After the Canon of the Roman Mass, the priest calls all to make confession, which is followed by the Absolution and Comfortable Words; then the Prayer of Humble Access, which is a good example of Cranmer's composition. The priest then receives Communion, and the people are to receive in both kinds immediately after him, which is a further innovation. The words of administration were taken from the service for the Visitation of the Sick but with the addition of the phrases 'given for thee' and 'shed for thee', which come from a Lutheran source. The service concludes with the Blessing.

If the *King's Primer* presaged things to come, much more so did the Order of Communion. It is to those 'things to come' to which we must now turn.

APPENDIX 1

THE PRIMER C. 1400 AD Contents

Kalendar

Matins
Psalms 8, 19, 24. Te Deum;
Lauds Psalm 93 Jubilate (Psalm 100);
Psalms 63, 148, 149, 150 all with Gloria
Benedictus with Gloria
Collects for Whitsunday, Trinity, for Peace

Prime
Psalms 54, 117, 118 'Hail Mary...'
Collects for Prime, of the Passion

Terce
'Hail Mary...' and opening versicles
Psalms 120, 121, 122
Collects of Terce, of the Passion

Sext
Opening versicles as at Prime
Psalms 123, 124, 125
Collect of Sext, and of the Passion
Psalms 130, Kyrie, Lord's Prayer

None (missing page in the MSS)
Psalms 120, 125, 126
Salutation to Mary

Vespers
Magnificat. Collects for Whitsunday, Trinity, for Peace of Vespers, of the Passion

Complin[e]
Psalms 13, 43, 129, 131
Nunc dimittis
Collects of the Annunciation, of the Passion

The Seven Psalms (of penitence)
Psalms 6, 32, 38, 51, 102, 130, 143

The Fifteen Psalms (Psalms of Ascent)
Psalms 120–134

Litany
Prayers to the Saints: Angels and Archangels; Priests and prophets; Apostles; Evangelists, disciples, holy innocents (x16); Martyrs (x14); Confessors (x14); 'by thy Incarnation...' Our Father...Hail Mary...prayer for the Church, our leaders, our bishop; for pity on our sins; that Christ's people may be holy and oned with us; for endless rest.

Placebo
Psalms 116, 120, 121, 130, 138, 146
Matins of the Dead – Psalms 5, 6,7, 119:73–80; 23, 25, 27.
The Burial Service – Psalms 40, 41, 42, 65, 63, 67, 148, 149, 150, 30 Lords' Prayer (x2)
The Commendation. Psalms 119:17–176,139

Psalms of the Passion
Psalms 22–31

THE KING'S PRIMER Contents

The Kalender

The King's Injunction
The Lord's Prayer
The Angel Gabriel's salutation to Mary

The Apostles' Creed

The Ten Commandments
Certain **graces** before and after meals

Matins
Ps 95, Hymn Pss 8, 19, 24,
Readings: from Isaiah 11, Luke 1
Te Deum

Lauds
Ps 67, Benedicite, Ps 148,
Benedictus
The Collects

Prime
Hymn, Ps 118, Collect of Prime

Terce
Hymn, Prayers

Sext
Hymn, Ps 123, Collect of Sext

None
Hymn, Ps 15, Collects for peace

Evensong
Pss 113, 135, 138, Hymn
Anthem , Magnificat, Anthem, Collect

Complin[e]
Pss 13, 43,
The Chapter, Hymn, Nunc dimittis
Collects.

The Seven (Penitential) **Psalms**
Pss 6, 32, 38, 51, 102, 130, 143

The Litany and Suffrages
omitting all prayers to the saints; concluding with the Prayer of St Chrysostom (Cranmer wrote it in 1544)

The Dirige or Vigil of the Dead,
Pss 116, 41, 146, Collects, Pss 5, 27, 42, Anthems, Readings from Job 2; John 6, Ps 71, Anthems and Prayers

The Commendations – Psalm 119

Psalms of the Passion (22, 69, 88, 2, 59)

The Passion of our Lord according to John.

Prayers of the Passion which may have been composed by Cranmer.

'**Certain Godly Prayers** for sundry purposes', e.g. for worthy reception of Communion, for Christ's Church, a lengthy prayer written by Erasmus, a general confession, for patience in trouble, 'In great trouble of conscience', 'Against pride', 'A prayer to be used at the hour of death', and the much-loved prayer 'O bone Jesu'.

Chapter 2

THE FIRST PRAYER BOOK OF EDWARD VI, 1549

CRANMER'S INTENTIONS: THE PREFACE TO THE 1549 PRAYER BOOK

In the medieval Church, there were five main service books. The Breviary contained the Divine Office – the eight daily Offices from Matins to Compline. The Mass was published in the Missal. The priest's services such as Baptism and Visitation of the Sick were printed in the Manual; services at which a bishop presided in the Pontifical. Finally, the Processional contained music for the processions on Sundays, Rogation Days and similar occasions. The use of these books was complicated for, as Cranmer wrote in the Preface to the 1549 Prayer Book, 'there was more business to find out what should be read, than to read it when it was found out'.

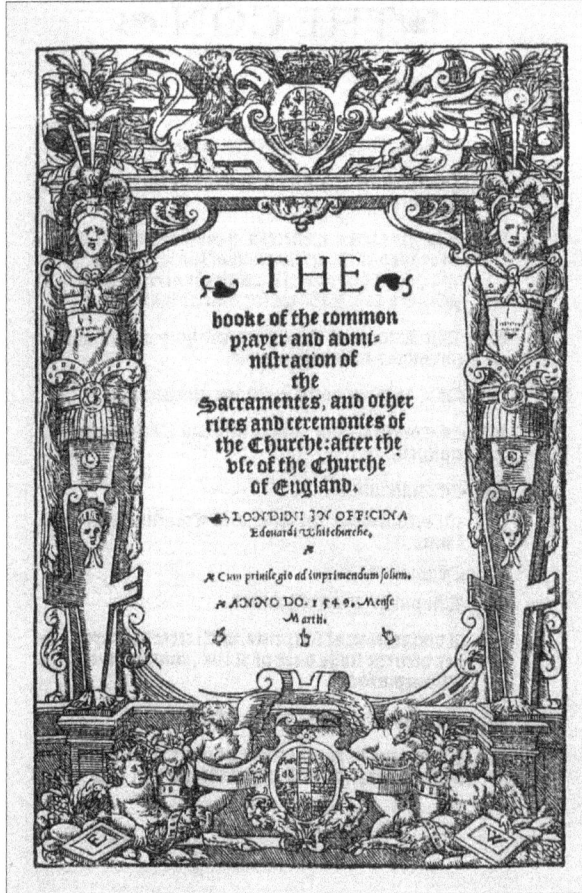

Plate 16. Title page of the 1549 BCP from a facsimile edition privately produced in 1896.

There was further variety and occasion for confusion because of different usages throughout the country. By the sixteenth century, there were five main 'uses': Sarum (Salisbury), York, Hereford, Bangor and Lincoln. However, the 'use' of Sarum predominated throughout the realm.

It was Cranmer's aim that worship should be contained in one book, in one common language and that 'from henceforth, all the whole realm shall have but one Use' thereby establishing uniformity through the land in the Church to which Henry had appointed himself the head.

Services in the vernacular was of primary importance to Cranmer. The Great Bible translated by Miles Coverdale had already been printed and distributed to every church in the land by Thomas Cromwell in 1538, and a chapter was to be read after the canticle at Matins and Evensong. By its daily use, Cranmer hoped that the Ministers would 'be stirred up to godliness themselves and be more able to exhort other by wholesome doctrine...and further that the people should...be the more inflamed with the love of true religion'.

The true religion to which Cranmer subscribed were the Reformed beliefs of the primacy of Scripture, justification by faith alone and every soul's direct access to the Father.

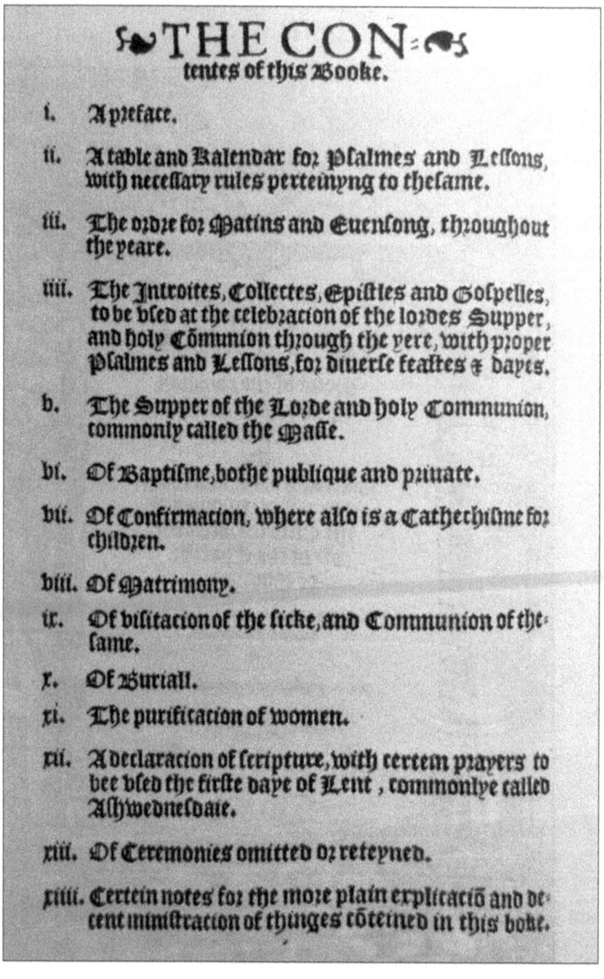

THE CON-
tentes of this Booke.

i. A preface.

ii. A table and Kalendar for Psalmes and Lessons, with necessary rules perteinyng to the same.

iii. The ordre for Matins and Euensong, throughout the yeare.

iiii. The Introites, Collectes, Epistles and Gospelles, to be vsed at the celebracion of the lordes Supper, and holy Cōmunion through the yere, with proper Psalmes and Lessons, for diuerse feastes & dayes.

v. The Supper of the Lorde and holy Communion, commonly called the Masse.

vi. Of Baptisme, bothe publique and priuate.

vii. Of Confirmacion, where also is a Cathechisme for children.

viii. Of Matrimony.

ix. Of visitacion of the sicke, and Communion of the same.

x. Of Buriall.

xi. The purificacion of women.

xii. A declaracion of scripture, with certein prayers to bee vsed the firste daye of Lent, commonlye called Ashwednesdaie.

xiii. Of Ceremonies omitted or reteyned.

xiiii. Certein notes for the more plain explicacio and decent ministracion of thinges cōteined in this boke.

Plate 17. BCP 1549 Contents page.

By radically simplifying the number of books required by both priest and lay people from five to two, the Bible and Prayer Book, Cranmer hoped that 'the people shall not be at so great charge for books as in the past they have been'. His aim was a better educated laity who would need only these two books for their profitable pursuit of the Christian life. The Injunctions of 1538 had required every incumbent to read the Bible that the laity might be better educated in it. The clergy were also to recite the *Paternoster*, Creed and Ten Commandments in English that lay people might learn them. His passion for education derived from his own person. The archbishop was one of the most learned men of his time. He read the Continental Reformers and besides Latin, Greek and Hebrew, read French, Italian and German. He was familiar with the early Church Fathers. His library at Lambeth Palace was more extensive than that of his own Cambridge University. He was familiar with the liturgies of the Churches of both the East and West. However, the Didache, the Apostolic Traditions of Hippolytus and the 'Sacramentary' of Serapion had not yet been discovered – texts which are of first importance to us.

THE PRAYER BOOK OF 1549: KALENDAR AND LECTIONARY

Cranmer's desire for a better theologically educated clergy and laity were expressed through the new Kalendar and Lectionary of the 1549 Prayer Book. His aim in devising the new Lectionary was that the whole Bible should be read over the course of the year and the Psalter over a month by using the new forms of Matins and Evensong. Each was assigned two passages of Scripture and each of those comprised a whole chapter, reading through a complete book of the Bible. The New Testament is read three times a year apart from the Apocalypse. Proper lessons are provided for saints' days and holy days. The Communion also included four passages of Scripture: Old Testament, Psalm, Epistle and Gospel. Eamon Duffy does not mince his words concerning the effect of this new provision:

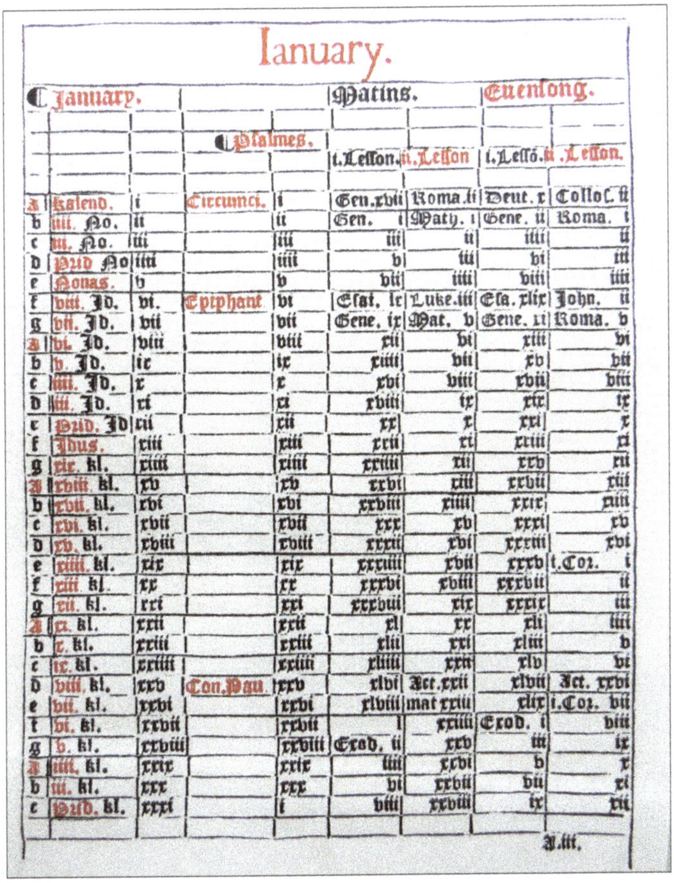

Ianuary.

January.				Psalmes.	Matins. i. Lesson.	ii. Lesson	Evensong. i. Lessō.	ii. Lesson.
A	Kalend.	i	Circumci.	i	Gen. xvii	Roma. ii	Deut. x	Collos. ii
b	iiii. No.	ii		ii	Gen. i	Math. i	Gene. ii	Roma. i
c	iii. No.	iii		iii	iii	ii	iiii	ii
d	Prid. No	iiii		iiii	v	iii	vi	iii
e	Nonas.	v		v	vii	iiii	viii	iiii
f	viii. Id.	vi.	Epiphani	vi	Esai. lx	Luke. iii	Esa. xlix	John. ii
g	vii. Id.	vii		vii	Gene. ix	Mat. v	Gene. xi	Roma. v
A	vi. Id.	viii		viii	xii	vi	xiii	vi
b	v. Id.	ix		ix	xiiii	vii	xv	vii
c	iiii. Id.	x		x	xvi	viii	xvii	viii
d	iii. Id.	xi		xi	xviii	ix	xix	ix
e	Prid. Id	xii		xii	xx	x	xxi	x
f	Idus.	xiii		xiii	xxii	xi	xxiii	xi
g	xix. kl.	xiiii		xiiii	xxiiii	xii	xxv	xii
A	xviii. kl.	xv		xv	xxvi	xiii	xxvii	xiii
b	xvii. kl.	xvi		xvi	xxviii	xiiii	xxix	xiiii
c	xvi. kl.	xvii		xvii	xxx	xv	xxxi	xv
d	xv. kl.	xviii		xviii	xxxii	xvi	xxxiii	xvi
e	xiiii. kl.	xix		xix	xxxiiii	xvii	xxxv	i. Cor. i
f	xiii. kl.	xx		xx	xxxvi	xviii	xxxvii	ii
g	xii. kl.	xxi		xxi	xxxviii	xix	xxxix	iii
A	xi. kl.	xxii		xxii	xl	xx	xli	iiii
b	x. kl.	xxiii		xxiii	xlii	xxi	xliii	v
c	ix. kl.	xxiiii		xxiiii	xliiii	xxii	xlv	vi
d	viii. kl.	xxv	Con. Paul.	xxv	xlvi	Act. xxii	xlvii	Act. xxvi
e	vii. kl.	xxvi		xxvi	xlviii	mat xxiii	xlix	i. Cor. vii
f	vi. kl.	xxvii		xxvii	l	xxiiii	Exod. i	viii
g	v. kl.	xxviii		xxviii	Exod. ii	xxv	iii	ix
A	iiii. kl.	xxix		xxix	iiii	xxvi	v	x
b	iii. kl.	xxx		xxx	vi	xxvii	vii	xi
c	Prid. kl.	xxxi		i	viii	xxviii	ix	xii

A.iii.

Plate 18. The Lectionary – January.

> The Calendar of the new book simply bulldozed away most of the main features of the liturgical year, leaving only the great feasts of Christmas, Easter and Whitsun (shorn of the octaves which extended and elaborated them), and a handful of biblical saints' days – the Apostles, the Evangelists, the Baptist, and Mary Magdalene. All but one of the feasts of the Virgin were abolished, including the great harvest celebration of the Assumption…At a more obvious level, the switch from Latin to English immediately rendered obsolete the entire musical repertoire of cathedrals, chapels and parish church. Not the least of the shocks brought by the prayer-book at Whitsun 1549 must have been the silencing of all but a handful of choirs and the reduction of the liturgy on one of the greatest festivals of the year to a monotone dialogue between curate and clerk.[i]

i Duffy, 2005[1992], p. 465.

THE PRAYER BOOK OF 1549: FROM EIGHT OFFICES TO TWO

One of Archbishop Cranmer's most significant and abiding achievements was the creation of two out of the eight monastic daily Offices. In monasteries, some of the Offices had already been combined, for instance, Matins and Lauds. Cranmer, who understood the impracticality of eight daily Offices for working people, nevertheless believed that every Christian should have the opportunity to pray daily and even unceasingly as the Apostle Paul recommended. The archbishop's solution was the two Offices of Matins and Evensong. He selected the elements from the eight monastic Offices: from Matins, the Lord's Prayer, versicles and responses, the *Venite*, and *Te Deum*; from Lauds, the *Benedictus*; from Vespers, the *Magnificat*; from Compline, the *Nunc Dimittis*. Collects were characteristic of every Office as is evident from the *Primers* (see Appendix 1), but in translating them from Latin, Cranmer gave them a distinctively English flavour.

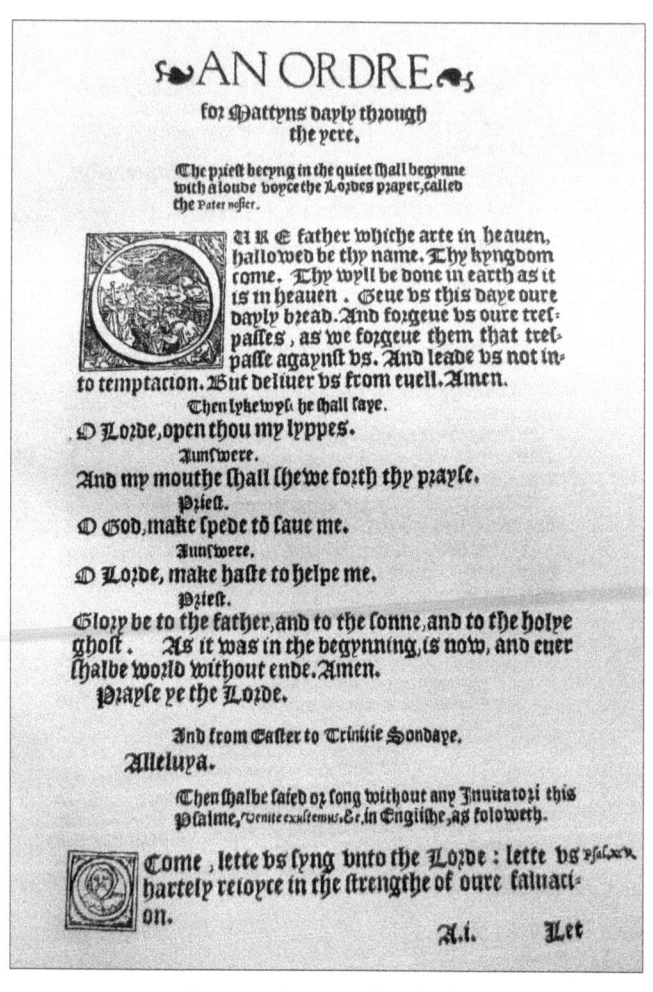

Plate 19. An Order for Matins daily through the year.

'An Order for Matins daily through the Year' has lasted the test of time:

> The Lord's Prayer called the *Paternoster* to be said in a loud voice.
>
> Opening versicles and responses concluding with the *Gloria*.
>
> The *Venite* (Psalm 95).
>
> The Psalms for the day from the new Lectionary.
>
> The set lessons, one from the Old Testament and one from the New. All to be read distinctly and in a loud voice or 'in such places where they do sing' they should be sung in a plain tune 'to the end the people may the better hear'.

The *Te Deum laudamus* to be said between the lessons except in Lent when the *Benedicite* is to be said.

The *Benedictus* follows the second lesson. All Psalms and canticles ending with the *Gloria.*

'Lord have mercy...Christ have mercy...Lord have mercy...'

The [Apostles'] Creed and Lord's Prayer in English with a loud voice.

Versicles and responses

The Collect for the Day, as appointed for the Communion, the Collect for Peace and the Collect 'for grace to live well'. The last two Collects to be said daily throughout the year.

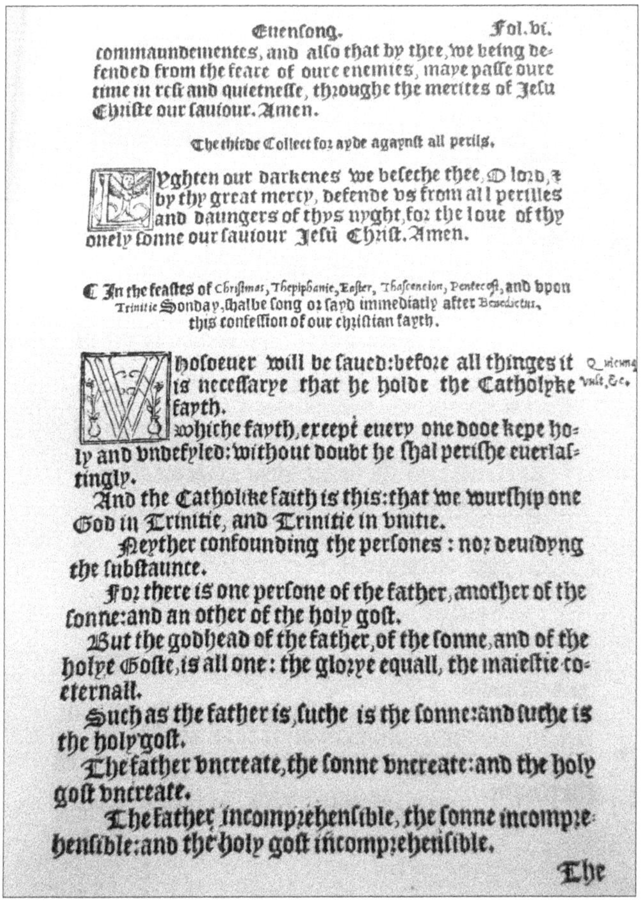

Evensong. Fol. vi.

commaundementes, and also that by thee, we being defended from the feare of oure enemies, maye passe oure time in rest and quietnesse, throughe the merites of Jesu Christe our saviour. Amen.

The thirde Collect for ayde agaynst all perils.

Lyghten our darkenes we beseche thee, O lord, & by thy great mercy, defende us from all perilles and daungers of thys nyght, for the love of thy onely sonne our saviour Jesu Christ. Amen.

In the feastes of Christmas, Thepiphanie, Easter, Thascencion, Pentecost, and upon Trinitie Sonday, shalbe song or sayd immediatly after Benedictus, this confession of our christian fayth.

Whosoever will be saved: before all thinges it is necessarye that he holde the Catholyke fayth. Quicunque vult, &c.

Whiche fayth, except every one doe kepe holy and undefyled: without doubt he shal perishe everlastingly.

And the Catholike faith is this: that we wurship one God in Trinitie, and Trinitie in unitie.

Neyther confounding the persones: nor devidyng the substaunce.

For there is one persone of the father, another of the sonne: and an other of the holy gost.

But the godhead of the father, of the sonne, and of the holye Goste, is all one: the glorye equall, the maiestie coeternall.

Such as the father is, suche is the sonne: and suche is the holy gost.

The father uncreate, the sonne uncreate: and the holy gost uncreate.

The father incomprehensible, the sonne incomprehensible: and the holy gost incomprehensible.

The

Plate 20. The conclusion of Evensong with the Second Collect and the beginning of Quicunque vult (the Athanasian Creed).

An Order for Evensong followed the same pattern. The appointed Psalms for the day succeeded the *Gloria, Magnificat* followed the first lesson from the Old Testament and the *Nunc Dimittis* the second lesson from the New Testament. The Collect for the day is succeeded by the Collect for Peace and the third Collect 'for aid against all perils'.

On the major festivals of Christmas, the Epiphany, Easter, the Ascension, Pentecost and upon Trinity Sunday, *Quicunque vult* (the Athanasian Creed) is to be said after the *Benedictus.* These festivals also have proper Prefaces in the Communion service and proper Psalms at Matins and Evensong.

These services of Matins and Evensong 'oscillate between praise and petition, gratitude and need'.[ii] One of the most memorable contributions Cranmer made to them were the Collects.

ii Jacobs, 2013, p. 31.

THE PRAYER BOOK OF 1549: THE COLLECTS

With the selection of Collects, Cranmer stuck closely to the Sarum rite for, out of the sixty-three Sarum prayers, all but eight are translations from the Latin. There are twelve new compositions. The second Collect of Matins is typical:

O Lord, our heavenly Father, Almighty and everlasting God, which hath safely brought us to the beginning of this day: Defend us in the same with thy mighty power; and grant that this day we fall into no sin, neither run into any kind of danger; but that all our doings may be ordered by thy governance, to do always that is righteous in thy sight; through Jesus Christ our Lord. Amen.

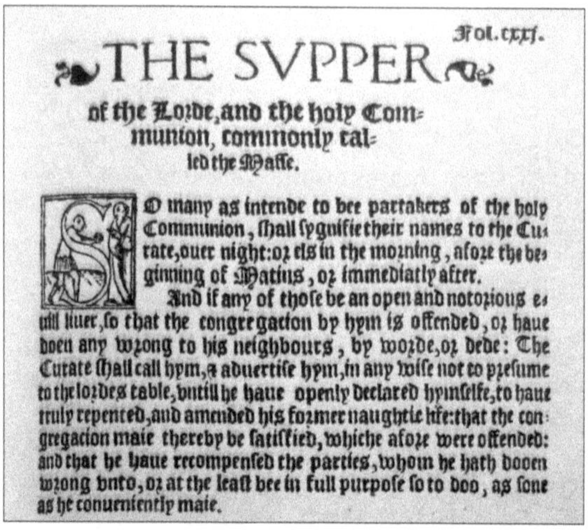
Fol. cxxi.

THE SVPPER

of the Lorde, and the holy Communion, commonly called the Masse.

SO many as intende to bee partakers of the holy Communion, shall sygnifie their names to the Curate, ouer night: or els in the mornyng, afore the beginning of Matins, or immediatly after.

And if any of those be an open and notorious euill liuer, so that the congregacion by hym is offended, or haue doen any wrong to his neighbours, by worde, or dede: The Curate shall call hym, & aduertise hym, in any wise not to presume to the lordes table, untill he haue openly declared hymselfe, to haue truly repented, and amended his former naughtie life: that the congregacion maie thereby be satisfied, whiche afore were offended: and that he haue recompensed the parties, whom he hath doen wrong unto, or at the least bee in full purpose so to doo, as sone as he conueniently maie.

Plate 21. THE SUPPER of the Lord and the Holy Communion commonly called the Mass.

Unity of thought characterises the prayer throughout. The first part begins with an acknowledgement of the nature of God's being, invoking his name, proclaiming the divine attributes and specifying what he has done for us. This is balanced by petition. Firstly, we ask that he may do something for us and secondly that we may respond appropriately. The ancient form of ending: 'through Jesus Christ, thy Son, our Lord, who liveth and reigneth with thee in the unity of the Holy Spirit, God for ever and ever' is shortened here. The balance between divine grace and human response is characteristic of Cranmer's Collects.

Some seventy of the Collects in the Prayer Book are translations of ancient Collects, some of which refer to human frailty

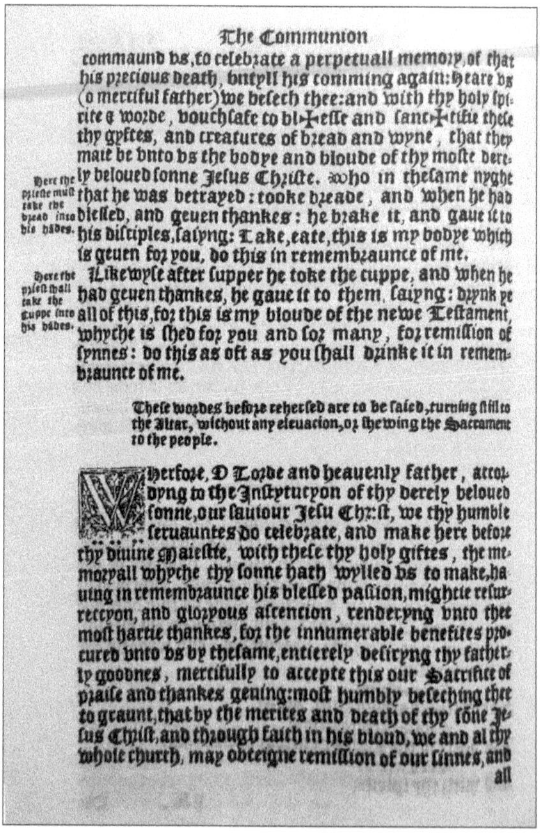
The Communion

commaund vs, to celebrate a perpetuall memory of that his precious death, untyll his comming again: Heare vs (o mercyful father) we besech thee: and with thy holy spirite & worde, vouchsafe to bl✠esse and sanc✠tifie these thy gyftes, and creatures of bread and wyne, that they maie be unto vs the bodye and bloude of thy moste derely beloued sonne Jesus Christe. Who in the same nyght that he was betrayed: tooke breade, and when he had blessed, and geuen thankes: he brake it, and gaue it to his disciples, saiyng: Take, eate, this is my bodye which is geuen for you, do this in remembraunce of me.

Here the priest must take the bread into his hādes.

Likewyse after supper he toke the cuppe, and when he had geuen thankes, he gaue it to them, saiyng: drynk ye all of this, for this is my bloude of the newe Testament, whyche is shed for you and for many, for remission of synnes: do this as oft as you shall drinke it in remembraunce of me.

Here the priest shall take the cuppe into his hādes.

These wordes before rehersed are to be saied, turning still to the Altar, without any eleuacion, or shewing the Sacrament to the people.

Wherfore, O Lorde and heauenly father, accordyng to the Instytucyon of thy derely beloued sonne, our sauiour Jesu Christ, we thy humble seruauntes do celebrate, and make here before thy diuine Maiestie, with these thy holy giftes, the memoriall whyche thy sonne hath wylled vs to make, hauing in remembraunce his blessed passion, mightie resurreccyon, and gloryous ascencion, renderyng unto thee most hartie thankes, for the innumerable benefites procured unto vs by the same, entierely desiryng thy fatherly goodnes, mercifully to accepte this our Sacrifice of praise and thankes geuing: most humbly beseching thee to graunt, that by the merites and death of thy sonne Jesus Christ, and through faith in his bloud, we and al thy whole church, may obteigne remission of our sinnes, and all

Plate 22. Consecration prayer with epiclesis and manual acts followed by the Prayer of Oblation with an anamnesis omitted in 1552.

recalling the Pelagian heresy and others the barbarian invasions of the same period when fear of enemies was widespread and deliverance natural and urgent. There are over thirty Reformation Collects, mostly saints' days, revised to avoid invocation of the saint. Cranmer's Collects are one of the least controversial elements of the new Prayer Book; the same cannot be said of the new service of Communion.

THE PRAYER BOOK OF 1549: HOLY COMMUNION

The title itself was unacceptable to the Reformers: *The Supper of the Lord, and Holy Communion, commonly called The Mass*. The result was that the word 'Mass' was dropped from the 1552 Prayer Book.

Among Cranmer's aims was that the service should be simple, scriptural and edifying. Hence, the service was in the vernacular with the emphasis towards corporate worship and away from the mediatorial role of the priest. There were two lessons only, an Epistle and Gospel, which were succeeded by a sermon, or one of the exhortations provided, which concluded the ministry of the word. A sermon or homily is to be delivered at the weekly celebration of holy Communion in contrast to the quarterly discourse recommended by medieval archbishops. The offertory commences the 'Liturgy of the Upper Room' because it is the people's freewill offering of bread and wine and for the poor of the parish. Over time, it became the offering of 'alms and oblations', 'alms' for the poor and 'oblations' for other purposes, notably the support of the ministry.

At the heart of the rite and succeeding the Offertory is the great prayer or Canon of the Mass commencing with the '*Sursum Corda*', Preface, *Sanctus*, based on Isaiah's vision in the temple (Isaiah 6:3), and the long consecration prayer, which begins with the prayer for the whole estate of Christ's Church. The consecration affirms Christ's death upon the cross as his 'one oblation once offered – a full perfect, and sufficient sacrifice'. No other priestly sacrifice is

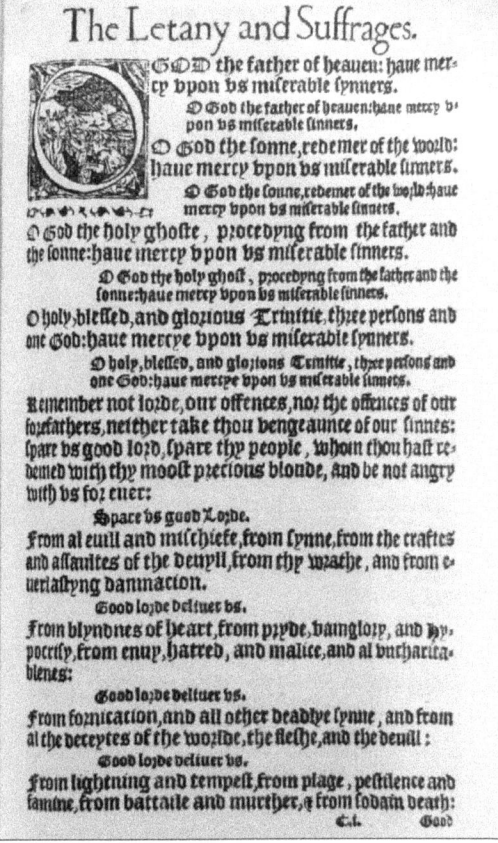

Plate 23. The Letany and Suffrages which follow Holy Communion.

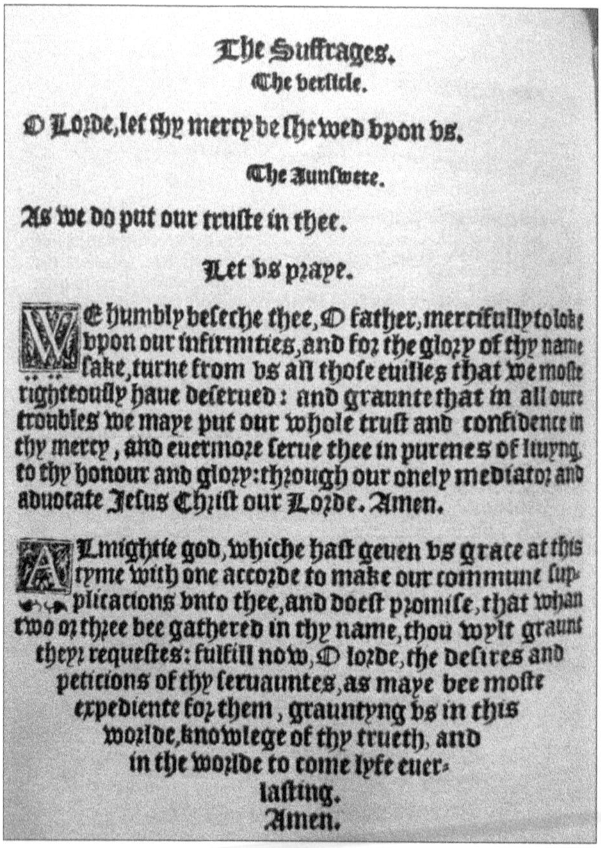

The Suffrages.

The verſicle.

O Lorde, let thy mercy be ſhewed vpon vs.

The Aunſwere.

As we do put our truſte in thee.

Let vs praye.

WE humbly beſeche thee, O father, mercifully to loke vpon our infirmities, and for the glory of thy name ſake, turne from vs all thoſe euilles that we moſte righteouſly haue deſerued: and graunte that in all oure troubles we maye put our whole truſt and confidence in thy mercy, and euermore ſerue thee in pureneſ of liuyng, to thy honour and glory: through our onely mediator and aduocate Jeſus Chriſt our Lorde. Amen.

ALmightie god, whiche haſt geuen vs grace at this tyme with one accorde to make our commune ſupplications vnto thee, and doeſt promiſe, that whan two or three bee gathered in thy name, thou wylt graunt theyr requeſtes: fulfill now, O lorde, the deſires and peticions of thy ſeruauntes, as maye bee moſte expediente for them, grauntyng vs in this worlde, knowlege of thy trueth, and in the worlde to come lyfe euerlaſting.

Amen.

Plate 24. The Letany concludes with the Prayer of St. Chrysostom.

necessary. Significantly, this prayer also contains an epiclesis – '*Hear us (O merciful Father) we beseech thee; and with thy Holy Spirit and word vouchsafe to bl+ess and sanc+tify these thy gifts and creatures of bread and wine…*' – an ancient element of Orthodox worship from the time of the *Liturgy of St Basil*. It was omitted in 1552. At the Words of Institution, the priest takes the bread and chalice into his hands still facing the altar but 'without any elevation or showing the Sacrament to the people'. As Brightman points out, the doctrinal basis of Cranmer's Canon is the threefold sacrifice, of our Lord on the cross, of praise and thanksgiving, and of ourselves; and only with reference to these offerings is any sacrificial language employed.[iii]

Importantly, the Prayer of Oblation which immediately follows begins with an anamnesis: '*we thy humble servants do celebrate and make here before thy divine Majesty, with these thy holy gifts, the memorial which thy Son hath willed us to make; having in remembrance his blessed Passion, mighty Resurrection, and glorious Ascension…*' Regrettably, these words were omitted in 1552. Nevertheless, there is an implicit anamnesis in the reformed Consecration prayer of 1552: '*…institute and command us to continue, a perpetual memory of that his precious death, until his coming again…grant that we receiving these thy creatures of bread and wine…in remembrance of his death and passion…*'. Yet there is no mention here of Christ's resurrection, ascension or coming in glory. No longer does the priest offer Christ's sacrifice but we offer a sacrifice 'of praise and thanksgiving' that 'we may obtain remission of our sins and all other benefits of his Passion'. Moreover 'we offer and present unto thee (O Lord) ourself, our souls and bodies, to be a reasonable, holy, and lively sacrifice unto thee'.

Cranmer hoped to satisfy the Reformers by omitting mention of oblation and to satisfy the conservatives by keeping the traditional framework and to provide a positive,

iii Cited in Cuming, 1969, p. 79.

Reformist-Catholic statement of what all had in common. Brilloth's comment on Luther may fit Cranmer aptly:

> ...throughout his life he retained a deep religious impression from the old Latin service, which his controversial writings indeed might seem to belie, but which never allowed him to lose hold of the element of mystery in the Eucharist, nor to break altogether with the traditional forms of the Church's worship.[iv]

This great prayer of intercession, consecration and oblation is succeeded by the Lord's Prayer and then the Preparation for Communion, invitation to confession, confession and absolution. To emphasise the Reformers' belief in justification by faith alone and to underline the righteous standing of the repentant sinner who has been absolved, the Comfortable Words follow and are succeeded by the Prayer of Humble Access, after which the priest receives Communion followed immediately by the people, who receive in both kinds.

During the Communion, the clerk shall sing 'O Lamb of God, that takest way the sins of the world; have mercy upon us' as well as, if necessary, a number of scriptural passages. The service concludes with the beautiful ancient prayer of Thanksgiving affirming our place in the Mystical Body of Christ and our inheritance through hope of his everlasting kingdom by the merits of his precious Death and Passion; and the Blessing.

Plate 25. The beginning of Matins in John Merbecke's *The Book of Common Prayer Noted.*

A summary of this nature cannot do justice to the beauty of Cranmer's language or the rich texture of its doctrinal elements. Much of this service was built upon the Latin rite of Sarum. Cranmer's purpose was to reform abuses, not to create a new religion. It is clear that he intended to repudiate the doctrine of Eucharistic Sacrifice, for the priest says at the end of the Canon: 'Christ our Paschal Lamb is offered up for us once and for all, when he bore our sins on his body on the Cross'. It is debatable whether he also rejected belief in the Real Presence. It seems to be implied by

---

iv Cuming, 1969, p. 81.

the rubric which states that *'every one (bread) shall be divided in two pieces... And men must not think less to be received in part, than in the whole, but in each of them the whole body of our Saviour Jesu Christ.'* However, he had already stated in the debate on the Prayer Book that: 'Our faith is not to believe Him (our Lord) to be in bread and wine, but that He is in heaven; this is proved by Scripture and Doctors.' And 'I believe that Christ is eaten with the heart. The eating with the mouth cannot give us life, for then should a sinner have life.'[v] All that has been omitted from the medieval rite is the invocation of saints, some of the ceremonial, notably the Fraction and Commixture, the complexity of its musical items and the prayers said silently.

The service was intended to be mainly choral. Parts to be sung included the Introit Psalm, *Kyrie, Gloria,* Creed, Offertory Sentences, *Sanctus, Agnus Dei* and the Post-Communion Sentence. The Epistle and Gospel are to be sung in a plain tune. Cranmer requested John Merbecke, a minor canon of Windsor, to write new settings providing one musical note for each syllable. In 1550, Merbecke issued *The Booke of Common Praier Noted*, in which he uses one or two simple Gregorian tones, though mostly it is newly composed. Merbecke directed the priest to intone the Canon (including the Preface) and the Prayer of Thanksgiving.

It has been argued that this service achieves a liturgy of 'almost perfect sequence [which] was broken in 1552 and has not been reinstated even in 1928',[vi] except that it has now been re-established in the recent liturgies of Common Worship. At the time, however, this rite did not please anyone. The conservative Bishop Gardiner claimed that the Prayer of Humble Access taught the doctrine of the Real Presence, and consequently, it was moved in the 1552 Book between the *Sanctus* and Prayer of Consecration and its wording slightly altered. Before an assessment is made of Cranmer's achievement in this first *Book of Common Prayer*, we must mention briefly the other services contained therein, for it was Cranmer's intention that only two books would be necessary for Christian discipleship, this one and the Bible.

THE PRAYER BOOK OF 1549: OCCASIONAL OFFICES

The medieval **Baptism** service was elaborate and set out in three parts: the making of a catechumen held at the church door and consisting mainly of exorcism, the blessing of the font and baptism. There was significant ceremonial; at the blessing of the font, the priest pours holy oil into the water and later anoints the child with the 'oil of salvation'. The child is baptised with threefold immersion

---

v Cited in Harrison, 1959, pp. 53-54.

vi Harrison, 1959, p. 63.

in the name of the Trinity. It is then anointed with oil (the Chrism), clothed with a white robe (Chrisom) and given a lighted candle.

Much of this pattern is retained in the 1549 Book. The preference is that Baptism should take place publicly at Easter and Whitsun, as was the practice in the early Church. Custom dictated more frequent use. At the church door, the priest prays that the child(ren) may be baptised with the Holy Ghost and made a member of Christ's Church and that 'by this wholesome laver of regeneration' sins may be washed away. The child's name is enquired and the sign of the cross made upon their head and breast. This is followed by a prayer of exorcism and a reading from the Gospel of Mark succeeded by 'a brief exhortation', after which all say the Lord's Prayer and Apostles' Creed. The priest then takes each child by the right hand in turn and leads them to the font. He first reminds the godparents of their responsibilities and then, having enquired the name of the child, puts six questions to the child, three to renounce the world, the flesh and the devil and three to affirm their belief in the Trinity using the words of the Apostles' Creed. After the child's name is pronounced a second time, the priest dips him/her into the water three times or if the child be weak pours water upon it. The godparents lay their hands upon the child, and the priest shall put upon him his white vesture commonly called the Chrisom. The priest then anoints the child upon the head, both actions performed with an appropriate prayer. Thereafter, the godparents are exhorted to teach the child the Creed, the Lord's Prayer and Ten Commandments. The children are to be brought to Confirmation as soon as they can recite the Articles of the Faith, the Lord's Prayer and the Ten Commandments. Provision is also made for 'Baptism in Private Houses in time of necessity'. In this way, Cranmer has kept

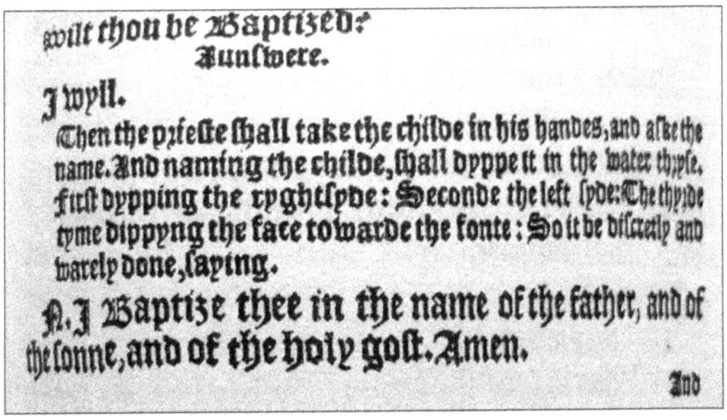
Wilt thou be Baptized?
Aunswere.
I wyll.
Then the prieste shall take the childe in his handes, and aske the name. And naming the childe, shall dyppe it in the water thryse. First dypping the ryghtsyde: Seconde the left syde: The thyrde tyme dippyng the face towarde the fonte: So it be discretly and warely done, saying.
N. I Baptize thee in the name of the father, and of the sonne, and of the holy gost. Amen.
And

Plate 26. The child is dipped in the water three times in Baptism.

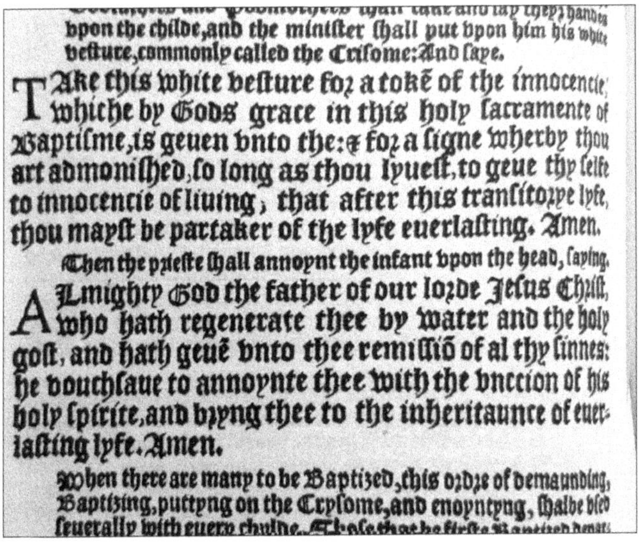
vpon the childe, and the minister shall put vpon him his white vesture, commonly called the Crisome: And saye.
Take this white vesture for a tokē of the innocencie, whiche by Gods grace in this holy sacramente of Baptisme, is geuen vnto the: & for a signe wherby thou art admonished, so long as thou lyuest, to geue thy selfe to innocencie of liuing, that after this transitorye lyfe, thou mayst be partaker of the lyfe euerlasting. Amen.
Then the prieste shall annoynt the infant vpon the head, saying.
Almighty God the father of our lorde Jesus Christ, who hath regenerate thee by water and the holy gost, and hath geuē vnto thee remissiō of al thy sinnes: he vouchsaue to annoynte thee with the vnction of his holy spirite, and bryng thee to the inheritaunce of euerlasting lyfe. Amen.
When there are many to be Baptized, this order of demaunding, Baptizing, puttyng on the Crysome, and enoyntyng, shalbe vsed seuerally with euery chylde.

Plate 27. The giving of the Chrisom robe and anointing in Baptism.

the essentials and preserved the structure while reducing the number of ceremonies and prayers.

Confirmation was rare and consisted of an anointing between two prayers. It is preceded by a Catechism of thirteen questions and answers, which the child was expected to learn 'before he be brought to be confirmed of the Bishop'.

'The Form of Solemnization of Matrimony' was little changed from the Sarum rite. 'Solemnization' was intended to indicate that this was a religious rite and not a civil contract but a 'holy estate [of life which] Christ adorned and beautified with his presence and first miracle that he wrought in Cana of Galilee'. To the two reasons for which matrimony was ordained, the procreation of children and for a remedy against sin, Cranmer introduces a third, 'for the mutual society help and comfort, that the one ought to have of the other both in prosperity and adversity'. It is reasonable to wonder whether this reflects the sensibilities of a married archbishop. To the bridegroom's and bride's words, Cranmer added 'to love and to cherish' just before 'till death us do part'.

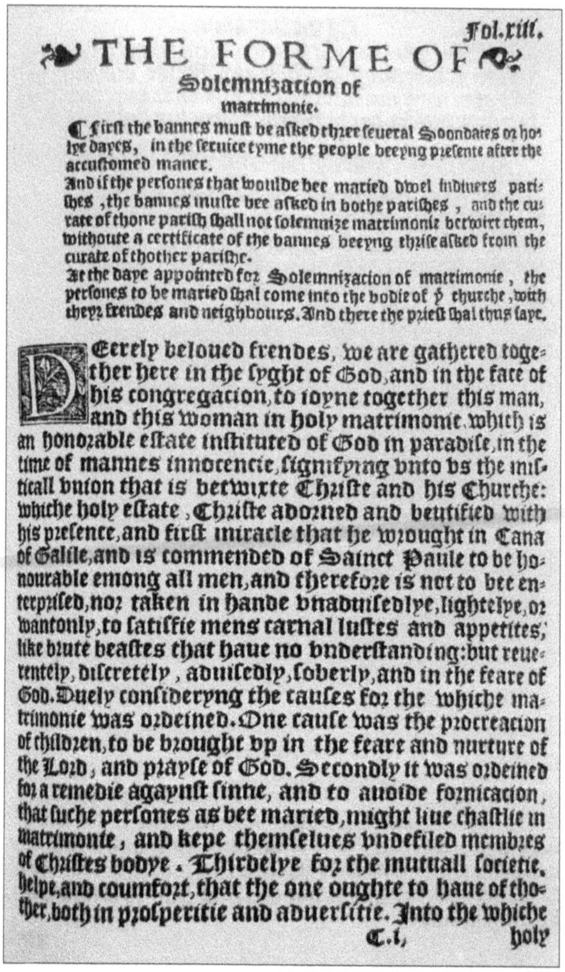
Fol.xiii.

THE FORME OF Solemnizacion of matrimonie.

First the bannes must be asked thre several Soondaies or holye dayes, in the seruice tyme the people beeyng presente after the accustomed maner.

And if the persones that woulde bee maried dwel indiuers parishes, the bannes muste bee asked in bothe parishes, and the curate of thone parish shall not solemnize matrimonie betwixt them, withoute a certificate of the bannes beeyng thrise asked from the curate of thother parishe.

At the daye appointed for Solemnizacion of matrimonie, the persones to be maried shal come into the bodie of ye churche, with theyr frendes and neighbours. And there the priest shal thus saye.

Deerely beloued frendes, we are gathered together here in the syght of God, and in the face of his congregacion, to ioyne together this man, and this woman in holy matrimonie, which is an honorable estate instituted of God in paradise, in the time of mannes innocencie, signifying unto us the mistical union that is betwixte Christe and his Churche: whiche holy estate, Christe adorned and beutified with his presence, and first miracle that he wrought in Cana of Galile, and is commended of Sainct Paule to be honourable emong all men, and therefore is not to bee enterprised, nor taken in hande unaduisedlye, lightelye, or wantonly, to satisfie mens carnal lustes and appetites, like brute beastes that haue no understanding: but reuerentely, discretely, aduisedly, soberly, and in the feare of God. Duely consideryng the causes for the whiche matrimonie was ordeined. One cause was the procreacion of children, to be brought up in the feare and nurture of the Lord, and prayse of God. Secondly it was ordeined for a remedie agaynst sinne, and to auoide fornicacion, that suche persones as bee maried, might liue chastlie in matrimonie, and kepe themselues undefiled membres of Christes bodye. Thirdelye for the mutuall societie, helpe, and coumfort, that the one oughte to haue of thother, both in prosperitie and aduersitie. Into the whiche

C.i. holy

Plate 28. The Forme of Solemnization of Matrimonie. Cranmer's third (new) reason for marriage at the bottom of the page.

The Order for the **Visitation of the Sick** and the Communion of the same was an especially important rite in an age of plague, frequent war and high child mortality. The Host was reserved for this purpose. The service opens with Psalm 143, and after suffrages and prayers, the priest exhorts the sick person to acknowledge that their situation is one of 'God's visitation' for whatever the cause, known or unknown. The sick person is reminded to forgive any offence, make amends for any wrongdoing, repay any debts, make a will and, if necessary, make special confession. The beautiful prayer of absolution which was also to be used in private confession has lasted the course of time:

Our Lord Jesus Christ, who hath left power to his Church to absolve all sinners which truly repent and believe in him: of his great mercy forgive thee thine offences: and by his authority committed to me, I absolve thee from all thy sins, in the name of the Father, and of the Son, and of the Holy Ghost. Amen.

This is followed by a prayer of renewal, Psalm 71, and an optional anointing on the forehead or breast with the sign of the cross in oil. The service concludes with Psalm 13. The focus of this rite is on the confession of sin and its absolution. What is missing and what was so central to the medieval rite were the symbolic gestures, particularly the priest's holding up before the dying person the crucified Christ on the cross. It was this symbolic action that prompted Julian's visions and her evocative Revelations.

The medieval **Funeral Service** was liturgically elaborate and very long. It was divided into four parts: Commemoration of Souls, Office of the Dead, Mass of the Dead, and Burial of the Dead. In all, during these rites, twenty-six Psalms and twenty-nine Collects were said, and the Lord's Prayer was repeated seven times. Cranmer's service is considerably shortened, consisting of three sections: procession, committal and service in the church. Cranmer anticipates the Anglican approach of finding the mean between the elaborate ceremonial of Sarum and the Continental Reformers' stark brevity. His service is also full of hope, opening with the sentence from John 11, 'I am the Resurrection and the life'. It concludes with a prayer that the deceased may 'ever dwell in the region of light', may rise with the just and righteous on the Day of the general Resurrection – the *dies irae* – and 'possess the kingdom which hath been prepared for you from the beginning of the world'.

Between them are the memorable words 'in the midst of life we be in death', and as the priest sprinkles earth upon the coffin, he commends the soul to God 'who shall change our vile body, that it may be like to his glorious body, according to the mighty working, whereby he is able to subdue all things to himself'. Psalms 116, 139 and 146 are read along with the whole of the fifteenth chapter of Paul's first letter to the Corinthians. Only the Collect, Epistle and Gospel for Holy Communion are printed as a separate service.

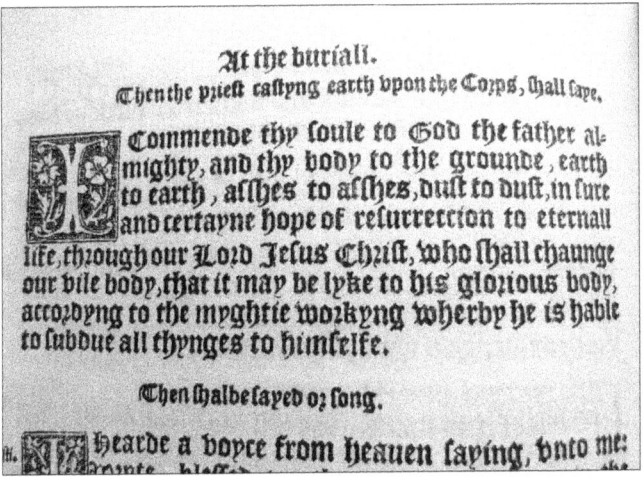

Plate 29. The priest addresses the soul in the 1549 funeral service.

All seven of the 'commonly called' sacraments were included in the *Book of Common Prayer* with the exception of **Ordination**. This was, however, quickly remedied and a new Ordinal attached to the Book a year after it was first published. The service provided is based on the Eucharist with an outline of the medieval service inserted in such a way that all three orders could be conferred in the same service, the deacons being 'ordered' after the Epistle, the priests after the Gospel and the bishops after the Creed.

Despite the many merits that Cranmer's first Book accomplished, it did not find a welcome reception; in fact, it pleased no one. It is possible to conjecture that Cranmer was conscious of the furore the new Book would create, as he includes an essay at the end, '**On Ceremonies why some be abolished and some retained**':

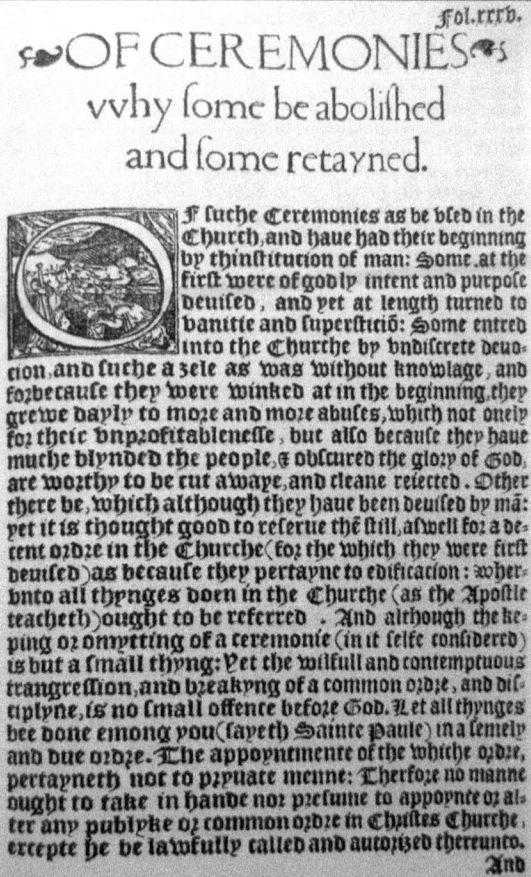

Plate 30. OF CEREMONIES why some be abolished and some retained.

Of such Ceremonies as be used in the Church, and have had their beginning by the institution of man, some at the first were of godly intent and purpose devised and yet at length turned to vanity and superstition...Others there be, which although they have been devised by man, yet it is thought good to reserve them still, as well for a decent order in the Church...as because they pertain to edification...Let all things be done among you (saith Saint Paul) in a seemly and due order...And moreover, they be neither dark nor dumb Ceremonies, but are so set forth that every man may understand what they do mean, and to which use they do serve.

This was Cranmer's intention, to abolish abuse and retain good order in worship, retaining those ceremonies which were edifying and whose use could be explained and understood. However, one man's abuse might be another man's piety, such is the nature of popular religion. Cranmer's edifying discourse did not satisfy opponents of the Book.

RECEPTION OF THE PRAYER BOOK OF 1549

The book was attacked from both sides. There was popular rejection and uprising in the West Country in 1549 and smaller disturbances from the Midlands to Yorkshire.

> The rebels sought a restoration not only of the old Mass, but of the full ceremonial range of medieval Catholicism. They singled out the sacramentals of holy bread and water, the Lenten ceremonies of ashes and palms, the parish procession on Sundays, but included 'all other ancient olde Ceremonyes used heretofore, by our mother the holy Church'.[vii]

Many of them were Cornishmen, who resented English authority and the imposition of the English language upon their traditional worship. The fact that they could not understand Latin either was beside the point, as they recognised that as the language of the universal Church. Their protests were silenced and the rebellion broken: as many as five thousand rebels were killed.

It was clearly not simply the change from Latin to English that upset the people but the removal of all references to Purgatory; praying for the dead by reciting their names, invocation of the saints, even the retention of altars, were all forbidden. Also forbidden was the blessing of lights at Candlemas, which would have evoked a stunning visual display of lights all around the church and, on Good Friday, kneeling at the cross placed before the altar. What antagonised the laity was the determination to stamp out 'immemorial devotional customs, even at the cost of preventing those who continued to use them from "taking their rights" by excluding them from Communion, effectively a re-definition of the community of the parish to include only the reformed.'[viii]

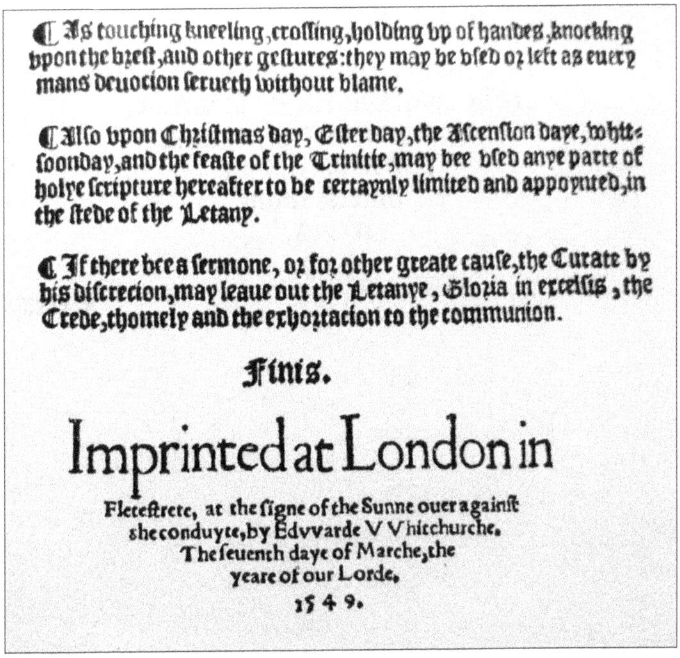

¶ As touching kneeling, crossing, holding vp of handes, knocking vpon the brest, and other gestures: they may be vsed or left as euery mans deuocion serueth without blame.

¶ Also vpon Christmas day, Ester day, the Ascension daye, whitsoonday, and the feaste of the Trinitie, may bee vsed anye parte of holye scripture hereafter to be certaynly limited and appoynted, in the stede of the Letany.

¶ If there bee a sermone, or for other greate cause, the Curate by his discrecion, may leaue out the Letanye, Gloria in excelsis, the Crede, the homely and the exhortacion to the communion.

Finis.

Imprinted at London in

Fletestrete, at the signe of the Sunne ouer against the conduyte, by Edvvarde VVhitchurche.
The seuenth daye of Marche, the yeare of our Lorde,
1549.

Plate 31. Final rubrics: about 'kneeling, crossing, holding up of hands, beating the breast and other gestures' that they are discretionary. Printed by Edwarde Whitchurche of Fleetstreet at the Signe of the Sunne, the 7th March 1549.

---

vii Duffy, 2005[1992], p. 466.

viii Duffy, 2005[1992], p. 467.

Neither did the Prayer Book of 1549 satisfy the Reformers. The Puritans mocked the use of the surplice, rejected the wafer in favour of ordinary bread, objected to the sign of the cross in Baptism, kneeling at Communion, the ring in marriage and bowing at the name of Jesus. Cranmer's Litany might well pray for deliverance from the 'tyranny of the Bishop of Rome and all his detestable enormities', but in their view, it would do no good to banish the pope only to repeat his worst crimes and errors. The priest still led worship from the choir, assuming a hierarchical position. He was called a 'priest' rather than a 'minister', and a priest's role was to preside at a sacrifice, so the word could imply that Christ was sacrificed again in each Mass. The Communion table was called an 'altar', again implying sacrifice, and the term 'Mass' was used in the title of the service.

The Reformers' party had been strengthened by a group of foreign Reformers brought to England by Cranmer as the nucleus of a Protestant Council. Bucer, who stood theologically between Luther and Calvin, was made Regius Professor of Divinity at Cambridge; Peter Martyr, who knew the Swiss Reformers, came to Oxford. They were joined by Hooper, later to become a bishop, and Coverdale and others like them who had fled to the Continent in the reign of Henry VIII. Although Cranmer was sympathetic to their views, being a convinced Reformer himself, it is debatable how much influence they had on the Prayer Book text.

What certainly did persuade Cranmer was the refusal of the Catholic side to accept the Prayer Book as a truly Reformed work and the determined attempt to interpret its language as consonant with pre-Reformation doctrines. For instance, the conservative Bishop Gardiner claimed that the Prayer of Humble Access taught the doctrine of the Real Presence.[ix] It was this attitude that convinced Cranmer that a new Book was required and that its language should be unequivocally Reformed.

---

ix Harrison, 1959, pp. 40, 66.

Chapter 3

THE 1552 REVISION AND THE ELIZABETHAN SETTLEMENT

PART ONE: THE 1552 REVISION

Cranmer had told Martin Bucer that the 1549 book was as far as he thought he could go in a reformed direction at the time. Bucer took this to mean that Cranmer's intention was always to produce a more reformed edition and that 1549 was only ever intended to be a halfway house. Although revision of the book was begun almost immediately, there is reason to think that Cranmer saw the 1549 book as striking a proper balance between traditionalism and reform.

In April 1552, a second Act of Uniformity was passed. In it, Cranmer praises the 1549 book as 'agreeable to the Word of God and the primitive Church, very comfortable to all good people desiring to live in Christian conversation' and explains that a new book is needed, not for 'any worthy cause' but 'because there has arisen in the use and exercise of the aforesaid common service in the Church, heretofore set forth, divers doubts for the fashion and manner of the ministration of the same.' As Jacobs points out, 'these do not seem to be the words of someone delighted to go forward towards the Continental models...but suggests a deep annoyance at being forced, under political pressure, to make unnecessary and largely cosmetic changes.'[i] That the changes were 'cosmetic' is highly debatable.

However, the view that Cranmer was pressured into making unwelcome changes challenges the scholarly con-

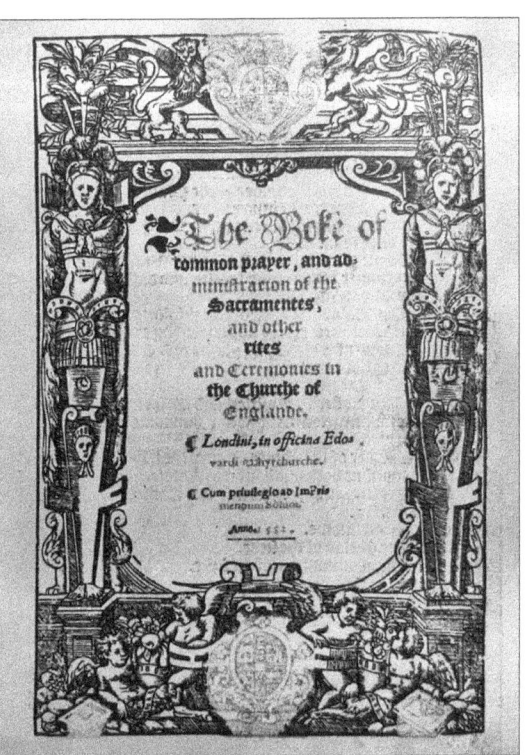

Plate 32. BCP 1552. Title page. From Ratcliff E.C. 1949 The Book of Common Prayer: its making and revisions 1549-1661. plate 42.

---

i Jacobs, 2013, p. 51.

sensus, first argued by Gregory Dix in *The Shape of the Liturgy*, that around 1546 Cranmer had undergone a conversion from a traditionalist view of the sacrament of Holy Communion to a fully Zwinglian one in which the rite is a memorial and nothing more. Dix sees the 1552 book as expressing Cranmer's truest beliefs. Jacobs accepts the narrative of Cranmer's conversion and acknowledges that Diarmaid MacCulloch, one of Cranmer's most recent and respected biographers, also accepts it but nevertheless questions its certainty, pointing out that Cranmer's only words on the matter are those referred to above.[ii]

The new book was authorised in April 1552 and brought into use on 1st November, All Saints' Day, of that year. Every passage cited by Bishop Gardiner as giving credence to traditional beliefs was either altered or removed. It was 'a determined attempt to break once and for all with the Catholic past, and to leave nothing in the worship of the Church of England which could provide a toehold for traditional ways of thinking about the sacred.'[iii] 'The words 'priest', 'altar' and 'Mass' are almost entirely eliminated throughout. At the same time, churches were being lime-washed throughout the country with the Royal Arms and texts from the Scriptures taking the place of the medieval wall paintings.

One element that Cranmer was not prepared to compromise on was the **Kalendar**, which followed the ancient pattern of the Church's year much as the Roman Church kept it.

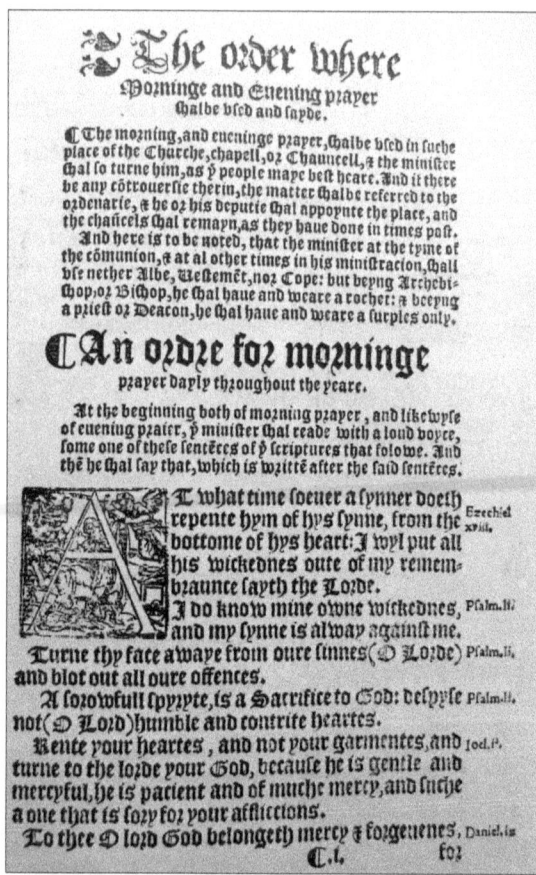

Plate 33. BCP 1552. The Order for Morning and Evening Prayer with the new 'Ornaments rubric' immediately above the Order for Morning Prayer. Ratcliff 1949 plate 43.

'Matins' and 'Evensong' now become '**Morning**' and '**Evening Prayer**'. The service is introduced by scriptural sentences. A paragraph of explanation leading into a prayer of confession and absolution reduces the need for private confession. Singular pronouns are changed to plural: 'O Lord, open thou *our* lips…O God, make speed to save *us*', emphasising the corporate nature of the service and discouraging individualistic

---

ii Jacobs, 2013, p. 209, note 4.

iii Duffy 2005[1992], p. 473.

piety. Psalm 100 was offered as an alternative to the canticle *Benedictus*. The Apostles' Creed, founded on the most ancient of all creeds, the old Roman baptismal Creed going back almost to the second century, now printed in full, is to be said by people and minister together instead of the priest on his own. The *Te Deum*, one of the glories of the Anglican Prayer Book, was maintained. In the Middle Ages, each Office had a hymn, and it is only through Cranmer's inability to write English verse that we are deprived of them.[iv] He said of himself: 'My English verses lack the grace and facility I would wish them to have.' Four new canonical prayers are added including one 'In time of any common plague or sickness'.

Plate 34. BCP 1552. Words of administration of Communion follow immediately after the institution narrative. Ratcliff 1949 plate 45.

The version of the Psalms that is used, because it had become familiar, is that of the Great Bible of 1539 translated by Miles Coverdale. This was regrettable because his translation was from the Latin and Greek versions and not the Hebrew.

It was the service of **Holy Communion** that received most radical revision. The words invoking the Holy Spirit to 'bless and sanctify' the bread and wine (the epiclesis) is now dropped together with the sign of the cross over the elements, which endorsed the notion that a powerful act of blessing was taking place. What had provoked the general misunderstanding of the 1549 Communion service was the retention of the traditional order of prayers of the canon of the Mass. It is to this rather than the words themselves that Cranmer applied radical alteration in order to bring about the doctrinal changes of 1552.

The Consecration Prayer is broken up with the insertion of the reception of Communion at its heart immediately after the Words of Institution precisely where in the old Mass the priest would have raised the consecrated elements to be seen by the people. Any possibility of adoration was thereby eliminated and the focus placed fully upon reception. It is no longer an

---

iv Harrison, 1959, p. 74.

explicit prayer for the consecration of the elements as it was in 1549, but a prayer that the faithful might be 'partakers of his most precious body and blood'. There is no 'moment of consecration' and no provision of manual acts from 1552 to 1662. The other elements of the 1549 Canon had now to be re-ordered. The prayer for the Whole Estate of Christ's Church, now 'militant here on earth', was placed immediately after the Offertory and shorn of any reference to prayer for the Saints or the departed except that we 'should follow their good examples'. The Confession and Comfortable Words come before the *Sursum Corda*. The Prayer of Humble Access was placed before the Consecration Prayer and the Prayer of Oblation after reception of Communion with the fine Thanksgiving Prayer an option to it, removing any possibility that these two prayers could be construed as implying a propitiatory sacrifice (i.e. a sacrifice to appease an angry God). The *Benedictus* is removed from the *Sanctus*. Most significantly, the words of administration are changed completely so that the elements are no longer called the Body and Blood of Christ. The focus is on receiving by faith in thanksgiving for Christ's death. The *Gloria* is moved from the beginning to the end of the service, ensuring that an element of the 'sacrifice of praise and thanksgiving' shall conclude the liturgy.[v] In the Gospels of Matthew and Mark, the narrative of the Last Supper concludes with the singing of a hymn.

Plate 35. BCP 1552. The 'Black Rubric'.
Ratcliff 1949 plate 47.

The presentation of the service and its visual impact was equally if not even more radical. The minister was now not allowed alb or cope but should wear a surplice like the parish clerk or the choir. The celebration should take place not at an altar but at a table set in the body of the church for audibility with a white linen cloth placed

---

v For a comparison of the structure of the 1549 and 1552 Communion services, see Appendix 2. See also Dix, 1964[1945], pp. 667–8.

upon it and with the priest standing on the north side. Ordinary bread was to be used, not wafers, which was to be placed in the hand and not the mouth as before. Any blessed bread left over after Communion was to be taken home for domestic consumption by the curate, thereby eliminating any notion of consecration. The sacrament would no longer be reserved or taken through the street for the sick excluding any chance to worship it. The priest had to celebrate afresh in the sick person's house with the one exception in time of plague. There had to be at least one other person present for a Communion service to take place. The Laity were to receive Communion at least three times a year, treble the number of the medieval rule.

There was one element upon which Cranmer stood firm, and that was the practice of kneeling at Communion. On this matter, he had a long and bitter argument with the ultra-radical Scot, John Knox. Knox argued that kneeling invoked reverence before a great lord and that therefore kneeling at Communion implied that the bread and wine had been transubstantiated into the Body and Blood of the Lord Christ. Cranmer found this argument ridiculous. Kneeling, in his view, was simply the acknowledgement of the dignity and seriousness of the occasion and that if the Reformers wanted to follow biblical precedent, they should receive the bread and wine reclining on one arm 'like Tartars and Turks today'.[vi] Eventually, a compromised was reached: the radicals would permit kneeling if Cranmer put in a disclaimer. This had to be printed separately and inserted

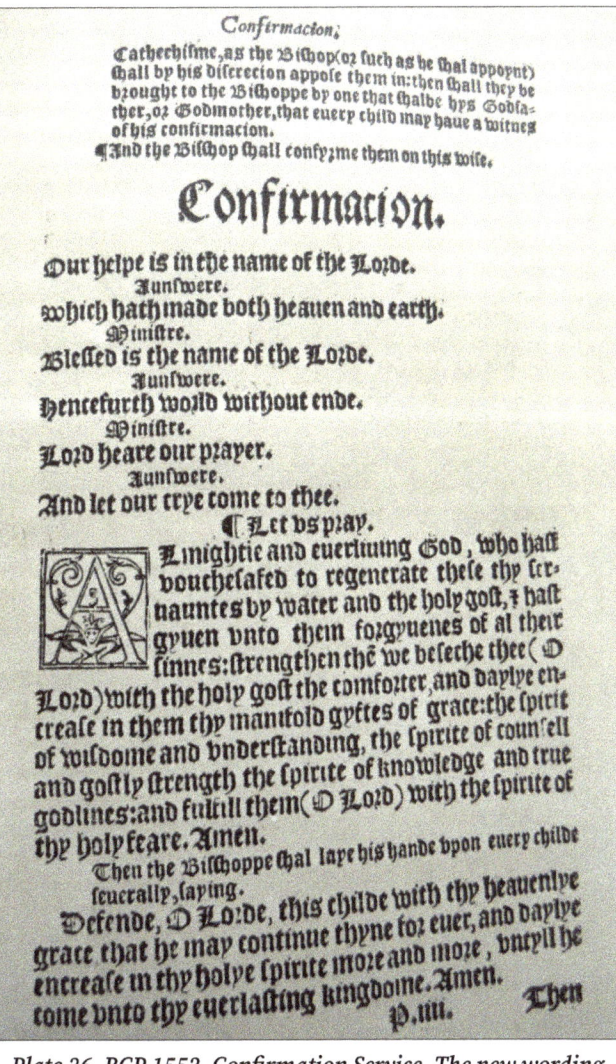

Plate 36. BCP 1552. Confirmation Service. The new wording changed the ancient traditional emphasis from 'completion' of Christian initiation to 'strengthening' the already initiated. Ratcliff 1949 plate 49.

---

vi Jacobs, 2013, p. 53.

later at the end of the service because the first copies had already come off the press. Unlike the other rubrics, which were printed in red ink, this was printed in haste in ordinary black ink, and a heavy type face was used and so it acquired the name the **Black Rubric**:

> ...Whereas it is ordeyned in the book of common prayer, in the administration of the Lord's Supper, that the Communicants knelyng shoulde recyue the holye Communion: whiche thynge being well mente, for a sygnificacion of the humble and gratefull acknowledging of the benefites of Chryst...Leste yet the same knelyng might be thought or taken otherwyse, we do declare it is not meant thereby, that any adoration is done...

Similar Reformist changes were made to the **Occasional Offices**. Anointing, exorcisms and the white Chrysom robe were discontinued from Baptism and the sign of the cross remained only here in the new Book. The whole service was to take place at the font, which was no longer to be blessed. The signing of the cross is removed from Confirmation. God is asked not to send down his Holy Spirit upon the candidates but merely to strengthen them with him. The celebration of Holy Communion was removed from the funeral service but retained for marriage. The funeral service itself was much altered. The whole service was to be said at the graveside. Lost is the notion of intercession for the dead person and the sense of communion between living and departed as the service becomes an exhortation to the living.

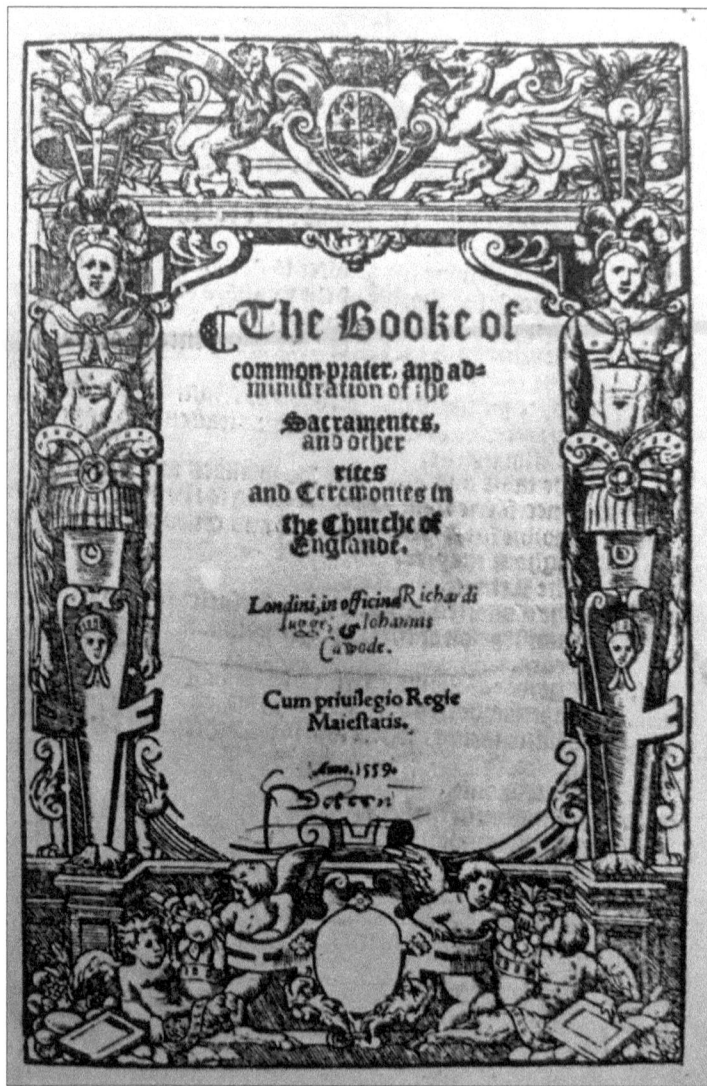

Plate 37. BCP 1559. Title page. Ratcliff 1949 plate 54.

The oddest thing about the 1552 burial rite is the disappearance of the corpse from it. So, at the moment of committal in 1552 the minister turns not towards the corpse, but away from it, to the living congregation around the grave. 'Foreasmuch as it hath pleased almighty God...we therefore commit his body to the ground...' Here the dead person is spoken not to (with the words 'I commend thy soul to God the Father Almighty') but about, as one no longer here...the boundaries of human community have been redrawn.[vii]

'The Purification of Women' is now renamed 'The Thanksgiving of Women after Childbirth', commonly called the Churching of Women, and takes place near the table instead of at the church door. The Ordination services are included in the book but still with their own title page.

CONCLUSION: CRANMER'S DOCTRINE OF HOLY COMMUNION

The remaining question is to ask whether the 1552 book truly expresses Cranmer's views or whether he was pressurised into making the changes. The Reformers' view was that since Christ's passion was wholly in the past, it can only be approached by a purely mental act of 'remembering' and imagination. Cranmer held this view since he said in answer to his own Visitation questions of 1547:

> The oblation and sacrifice of Christ in the Mass is so called not because Christ indeed is there offered and sacrificed by the priest and the people...but it is so called, because it is a memory and representation of that very true sacrifice and immolation which before was made upon the cross.[viii]

In his defence at his trial, Cranmer affirms a spiritual eating and drinking reminiscent of the words of the Gospel of John chapter six:

> (The words[...]'He that eateth My flesh etc.') '...are not to be understand[ed] that we shall eat Christ with our teeth grossly and carnally, but that we shall spiritually and ghostly with our faith eat him, being carnally absent from us in heaven; and *in such wise as Abraham and other holy fathers did eat him* many years before He was incarnated and born...'

> [Further...]'The true eating of Christ's very Flesh and drinking of His Blood' is '...an inward, spiritual and pure eating with heart and mind; *which is to believe in our hearts that His Flesh was rent and torn for us upon the cross and His Blood shed for our redemption*, and that the same Flesh and Blood now sitteth at the right hand of the Father, making continual intercession for us[...]'[ix]

> '...His holy supper was ordained for this purpose, *that every man eating and drinking thereof should remember that Christ died for him, and so should exercise his faith,*

---

vii Duffy, 2005[1992], p. 475.

viii Dix, 1964[1945], p. 641.

ix Dix, 1964[1945], p. 648.

and comfort himself by the remembrance of Christ's benefits; and so give unto Christ most hearty thanks and give himself unto Him.'[...]

'Consecration is the separation of any thing from a profane and worldly use unto a spiritual and godly use...' [and the bread and wine cannot] '[...]be partakers of any holiness or godliness or can be the Body and Blood of Christ; but[...]they *represent* the very body and blood of Christ[...]And so they can be called by the names of the Body and Blood of Christ, as the *sign*, *token* and *figure* is called of the very thing which it showeth and signifieth.'[x]

Although Cranmer does appear to have had a Zwinglian[xi] view of the Eucharist with regard to his abhorrence of the sacrificial aspect of the Mass, he nevertheless seems to have had a more nuanced belief in the spiritual presence of Christ. Two considerations suggest this: firstly, he believed that the 1549 rite was radically different from the Mass and that it was consistent with the doctrine of 'justification by faith alone'; and secondly, he affirmed '*that Christ is in all persons* that truly believe Him in such sort that with His Flesh and Blood He doth spiritually nourish and feed them and giveth them everlasting life, and doth assure them thereof, *as well by the promises of his Word*, as by the sacramental Bread and Wine in His holy supper'.[xii] To believe that the spiritual presence of Christ is in the believer and the words of Scripture as well as the Bread and Wine of Holy Communion suggests a richly textured understanding of that presence, which a purely Zwinglian understanding of Cranmer's doctrine fails to do justice.

Plate 38. BCP 1559. The title page of the English Litany with the anti-papal petition removed. Ratcliff 1949 plate 53.

---

x   Dix, 1964[1945], pp. 650–1.

xi 'For Zwingli, therefore, the sacrament shifted in meaning from something God did for humanity, to something which humanity did for God.' (MacCulloch, 2009, p. 621).

xii MacCulloch, 2009, p. 651. Emphasis added.

Had Cranmer lived another eighty years, he might have rejoiced to see the publication of the 1637 book, which incorporated many of the elements from the primitive Orthodox liturgies whose place he had maintained in the 1549 Prayer Book. The story of that later book will be told in the following chapter, but before doing so, the Elizabethan Settlement must be recounted.

PART TWO: THE ELIZABETHAN SETTLEMENT

Edward VI died on 6th July 1553, giving the 1552 Prayer Book only nine months' use. After the debacle of Lady Jane Grey, Edward's elder sister Mary had ascended the throne by September of that year. Many of the Evangelicals fled to the Continent, as Mary reimposed traditional Catholicism. Cranmer sent his wife and family abroad but remained himself where he was burned at the stake on Oxford Broad Street on 20th March 1556. Mary's reign was even shorter than her brother's had been. She died on 17th November 1558. The sympathies of her younger sister Elizabeth, who succeeded her, were with the Protestants. Elizabeth's preference was with the 1549 book, but William Cecil, her astute adviser, persuaded her that it would be more politic to adopt the 1552 edition. She did so but with significant changes.

Elizabeth's aim and that of her court was to achieve a settlement that would

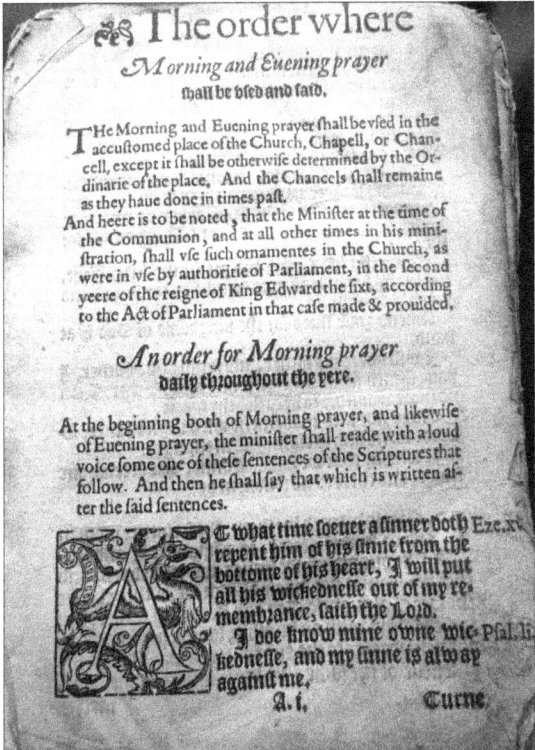

Plate 39. Elizabethan BCP. Title page of Morning Prayer with revised 'Ornaments rubric'.

Plate 40. Elizabethan BCP. Venite Creator (Psalm 95) pointed.

ensure no invasion from Spain or France and deter any reversion back to papal authority. A new supremacy bill was completed by April 1559, which styled the monarch as 'supreme governor' of the Church rather than 'supreme head'. Attached to it was yet another Act of Uniformity authorising the altered Prayer Book of 1552.

A rubric placed at the beginning of Morning Prayer authorised the minister to 'use such ornaments in the Church, as were in use by authority of Parliament, in the second year of the reign of King Edward the Sixth'. This appeared to sanction those vestments such a cope and chasuble and ornaments such as candles and altars that were accepted in the first Prayer Book of 1549. It became known as the **Ornaments Rubric** and was invoked by the High Church party in the nineteenth century, causing much controversy. The prayer that we might be delivered from the 'tyranny of the Bishop of Rome and all his detestable enormities' was removed from **the Litany**. Prayers were added at the end of the Litany including the text of 2 Corinthians 13:14 which we now call 'the Grace'.[xiii] There were also other ways in which the Elizabethan Settlement was sympathetic to Catholic sensibilities; for instance, the Rogationtide procession was restored as a religious thanksgiving for the fruits of the earth and a means of preserving boundaries.[xiv]

Plate 41. Elizabethan BCP.
The Lord's Prayer pointed.

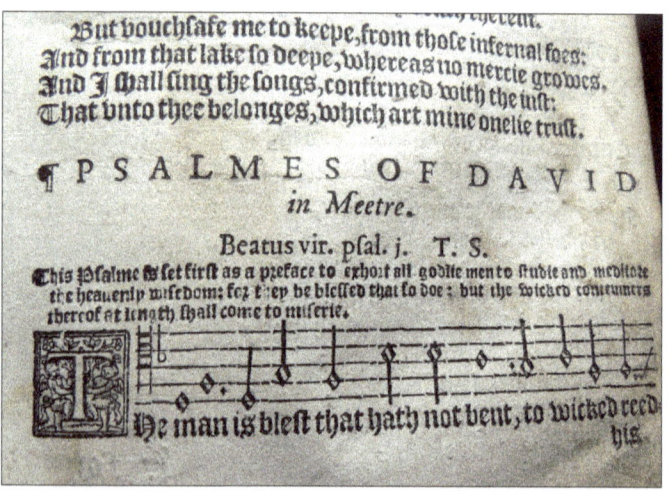

Plate 42. Elizabethan BCP. The Psalms of David in metre.

xiii Cuming, 1969, p. 123.

xiv Duffy, 2005[1992], p. 568.

The **Black Rubric** at the end of **Holy Communion** was removed and did not reappear in the Prayer Book until 1662. Perhaps most significantly, the **words of administration** of the sacrament of the Lord's Body and Blood were altered to include those of 1549 with the new words of 1552. This has positive value in so far as the combined words emphasise both the self-giving of the Lord and explicitly state the demands upon the worshipper. In 1561, fifty-seven saints' days reappeared in the Calendar, and the 1551 edition of King Henry's *Primer* of 1545 was reissued in 1559, suggesting conservative and Catholic sympathies.

Plate 43. Elizabethan BCP.
Jubilate Deo – Psalm 100 with familiar 'Old Hundredth' tune.

Due to the scarcity of educated pastors, 'certain sermons or homilies' were published 'to be read by the curates of mean understanding...upon the sabbath days unto the congregation'.[xv] Cranmer's aspiration of daily Morning and Evening Prayer and weekly Holy Communion remained exactly that. In many parishes, Communion became a monthly, quarterly or even triannual celebration, and the main Sunday service of the Elizabethan Church was Morning Prayer, the Litany and the first part of the Communion service with a sermon and Evening Prayer with catechism. A further book was added to the **Book of Homilies** in 1563, which was the service for the anniversary of the Queen's accession, first used in 1576 and repeated yearly thereafter.[xvi]

Thomas Tallis and William Byrd were the best-known **musicians** of the Elizabethan Church, and they provided music for the new English services. Interestingly, they both worked across religious divides. Tallis served both Mary and Elizabeth quite happily, and Byrd was a definite Roman Catholic recusant! The lead in metrical Psalmody was taken by Miles Coverdale and Thomas Sternhold. Sternhold published nineteen metrical Psalms in 1547/48 under the title *Certayne Psalmes*. He died in 1549, but eighteen more of his publications were published posthumously together

---

xv Spinks, 2017, p. 12.

xvi Cuming, 1969, p. 124.

with the original eighteen by Edward Whitechurch under the title *Al such Psalmes of Dauid as Thomas Sternehold late grome of y[e] kinges Maiesties Robes, didde in his life time draw into English Metre*. This book included a further seven psalms by John Hopkins.[xvii] The choir was positioned in the musicians' gallery at the west end. Stalls were provided in the chancel for communicants, pews in the nave for the other services, the font remaining in its ancient place by the door.

The doctrinal basis of the Settlement was indicated by the appearance of the 'Forty-Two Articles' of 1553, reduced to thirty-eight in 1563, finally reaching their familiar number of thirty-nine in 1571.[xviii]

Inevitably, Protestant divines found fault with the 1559 book and agitated for reform but had no success. It was stoutly defended by Richard Hooker in his *Laws of Ecclesiastical Polity* which remained the standard work of apologetics for the Elizabethan Settlement. Judith Maltby[xix] has shown how by the end of Elizabeth's long reign most English people had become devoted to the new English Prayer Book and had absorbed its spirituality. Duffy would agree: 'Cranmer's sombrely magnificent prose, read week by week, entered and possessed their minds, and became the fabric of their prayer, the utterance of their most solemn and their most venerable moments.'[xx]

[xvii] Spinks, 2017, pp. 19–20.
[xviii] Cuming, 1969, p. 130.
[xix] Maltby, 1998.
[xx] Duffy, 2005[1992], p. 593.

APPENDIX 2

1549 BCP HOLY COMMUNION	1552 BCP HOLY COMMUNION
THE ORDER	THE ORDER
The Lord's Prayer	
Collect for Purity	Collect for Purity
Psalm appointed for the introit	Ten commandments
Gloria	
Greeting	
Collect of the Day	Collect of the Day
One of two Collects for the King	One of two Collects for the King
Epistle	Epistle
Gospel	Gospel
Nicene Creed	Nicene creed
Sermon/homily	Sermon or homily or Exhortation (as set)
Exhortation to those minded to receive Communion	Notices and offertory sentence
Exhortation to regular Communion	The collection
Offertory – with Scripture sentence(s)	Prayer for the whole estate of Christ's Church
Sursum Corda	Exhortation to regular Communion
Proper Preface (if appropriate)	(additional Exhortation at the priest's discretion)
'Therefore with angels...'	Exhortation to come to Communion worthily
Sanctus with Benedictus	Invitation to confession
Prayer for the whole estate of Christ's Church	General confession
Prayer of [consecration] with epiclesis with sign of the cross and Dominical Words, taking the bread and cup into his hands	Absolution
	Comfortable Words
	Sursum Corda
	Proper Preface
	'Therefore with angels...'
	Prayer of Humble Access
'Memorial' prayer – 'Wherefore, O Lord and heavenly Father...' (without any elevation or showing the sacrament to the people)	Prayer of (consecration without epiclesis) 'that we...receiving this bread and wine...in remembrance of his passion and death, may be partakers of his most precious body and blood...'
The Lord's Prayer	Priest and people receive Communion: 'Take and eat this in remembrance that Christ died for thee, and feed on him in thy heart by faith with thanksgiving.'
'Christ our Paschal Lamb is offered up for us...'	
Invitation to confession	
Prayer of confession	
Absolution	
Comfortable Words	
Prayer of Humble Access – by priest kneeling	Lord's Prayer with the people repeating after the priest.
Priest then people receive Communion: 'The body of our Lord Jesus Christ which was given for thee, preserve thy body and soul unto everlasting life.'	'O Lord and heavenly Father, we desire thy fatherly goodness mercifully to accept this our sacrifice of praise and thanksgiving...' OR Prayer of Thanksgiving
Agnes Dei (short)	
Post Communion sentences sung by the clerks	
Prayer of Thanksgiving	Gloria
Blessing (Peace and blessing)	Blessing by priest or bishop.

Chapter 4

THE EARLY STUARTS

JAMES I AND VI, THE MILLENARY PETITION, THE HAMPTON COURT CONFERENCE, AND THE GODLY

Elizabeth died childless on 24th March 1603. The throne passed to the rightful heir and son of Mary Queen of Scots, James VI of Scotland. On his way south, James was presented with the **Millenary Petition** by a considerable number of Puritans known also as 'the godly'. (The name 'Puritan' was applied to those who were dissatisfied with the Elizabethan Settlement of 1559. They sought further purification of the Church along the Geneva model.) Their main criticism of the Prayer Book was that reading prayers were formal and do not touch the heart. They also demanded several other things which they considered smelt of Rome: the use of the words 'priest' and 'altar', the suggestion that ministers were empowered to pronounce absolution from sin, the use of special clerical costumes and the signing of the cross in Baptism. But what they really wanted was the abolition of the Prayer Book. Some also had anti-episcopal sympathies.[i]

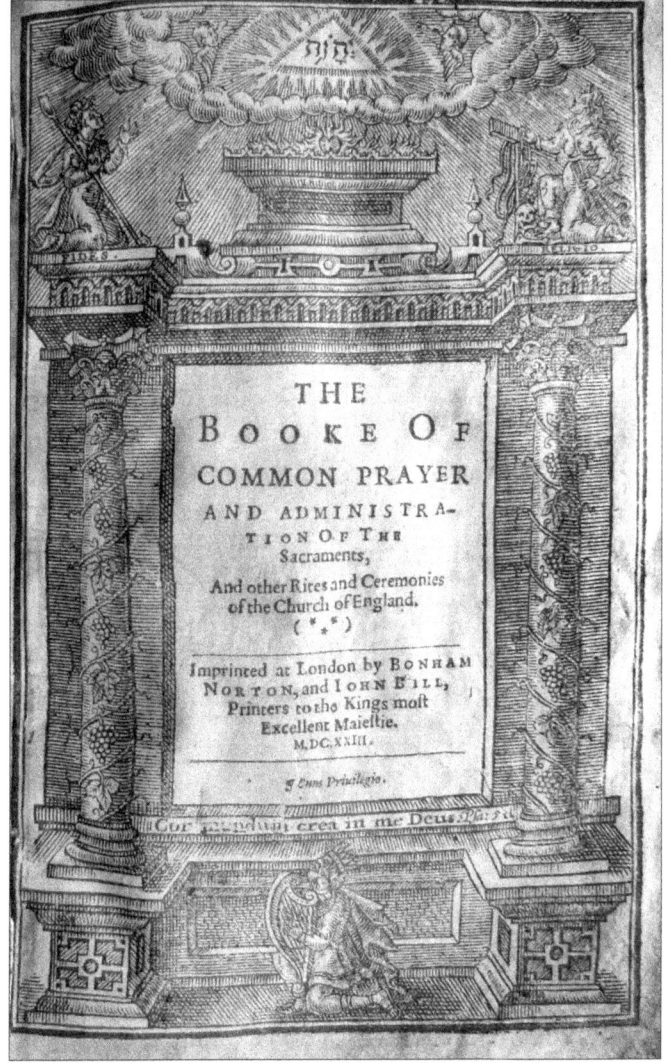

Plate 44. Title page of a 1623 BCP
Printed by Bonham Norton and John Bill,
printers to the King's most Excellent Majesty. MDCXXIII.

---

i Jacob, 2013, p. 69.

James neither accepted nor rejected the petition but called a Conference, which met at **Hampton Court** in January 1604. Eight bishops, seven deans and two doctors of divinity represented the established Church; the Puritans were allowed four speakers. James confined the Conference to six points, three directly concerning the Prayer Book: the general absolution, confirmation of children and private baptism by women.

After only three days of discussion, it was agreed that the words pronouncing remission of sins should be added to the absolution, that the word 'catechising' be

Plate 45. BCP 1623. First page of the genealogies beginning with God (Luke 3:38).

added to Confirmation, that only ministers and curates should administer private baptism excluding women and midwives (a particular concern of the godly), that a section on Baptism and Communion be added to the Catechism, that Old Testament passages replace four from the Apocrypha, and most importantly that a new translation be made of the whole Bible. This final decision was put into immediate effect, and the work concluded with the publication of the Authorised Version in 1611. Further minor additions include a prayer for the Royal Family at Matins and Evensong and a suffrage for them in the Litany. Prayers were also provided for rain, fair weather,

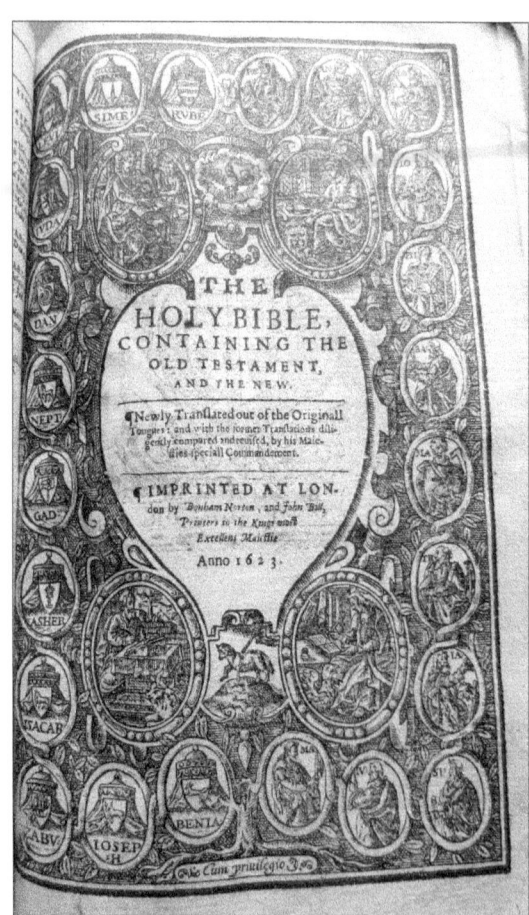

Plate 46. Title page of the Bible in the 1623 BCP. The tents of the sons of Jacob are on the left side.

thanksgiving for plenty, for peace and victory and deliverance from the plague.

A new version of the Canons was enacted in March 1604. These enforced the wearing of the surplice and required a church to have a stone font, a decent Communion table covered with a carpet of silk and a fair linen cloth at the time of the service, the Ten Commandments on the east wall with other chosen texts, a pulpit, a chest for alms, a Bible and Prayer Book and the Table of Prohibited Degrees of Marriage. Communion was to be received three times a year, and the words of Institution had to be used over any additional bread

Plate 47. The eye of God observing Guy Fawkes entering the Houses of Parliament; introducing the service of Thanksgiving for the 'happy deliverance of the King and the Three Estates of the Realm from the most Traitorous and bloody intended Massacre by gunpowder', from a BCP of 1685.

or wine brought to the table, 'reconsecration' being required by canon law. Canon 30 robustly defended the use of the sign of the cross in Baptism. In such manner the Jacobean Settlement was complete.[ii]

The discovery of Guy Fawkes' 'most traitorous and bloody-intended massacre by gunpowder' impacted the mind of the nation and initiated a service of deliverance of Parliament to be held

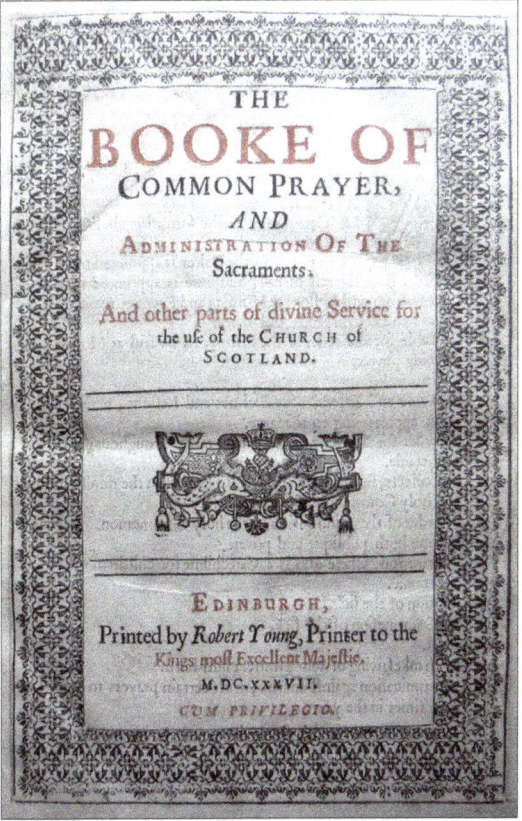

Plate 48. Title page of the 1637 Scottish BCP. Printed in Edinburgh by Robert Young, Printer to the King's most Excellent Majesty MDCXXXVII.

---

ii Cuming, 1969, pp. 137–139.

annually on 5th November from 1606. It was an amended form of Morning Prayer with Psalms, special suffrage and Collects.

THE RISE OF PATRISTIC REFORMED CHURCHMEN

While the godly wanted further reform of the Church of England and the Prayer Book, a more conservative and Catholic group were gaining attention and positions of authority. They took their inspiration more from patristic sources than Reformation ones and, like Elizabeth I, preferred the 1549 Book to that of 1552. Leading lights of this group were Bishops Lancelot Andrewes, John Overall (of Norwich) and John Buckeridge. Andrewes argued that the sermon was not the most important part of worship, that Evensong should be kept on Saturdays and a fast before saint days. One of his followers, Richard Neile, was appointed Bishop of Durham in 1617, and he surrounded himself with younger protégés, including John Cosin and William Laud. They became known as 'Laudians' and were concerned with royal authority, episcopacy, the sacraments and the beauty of holiness in worship, with lavish expenditure on copes, frontals, woodwork and fine bindings.[iii] The Laudians were prepared to conserve the Prayer Book intact.

In 1617, William Laud, as bishop of Gloucester, ordered the Communion tables to be moved to the east end of the cathedral claiming that he was following the practice of the Chapel Royal. Later, as archbishop, Laud insisted that all altars should be placed against the east wall of the chancel and surrounded with a rail to ensure both that the communicants should kneel to

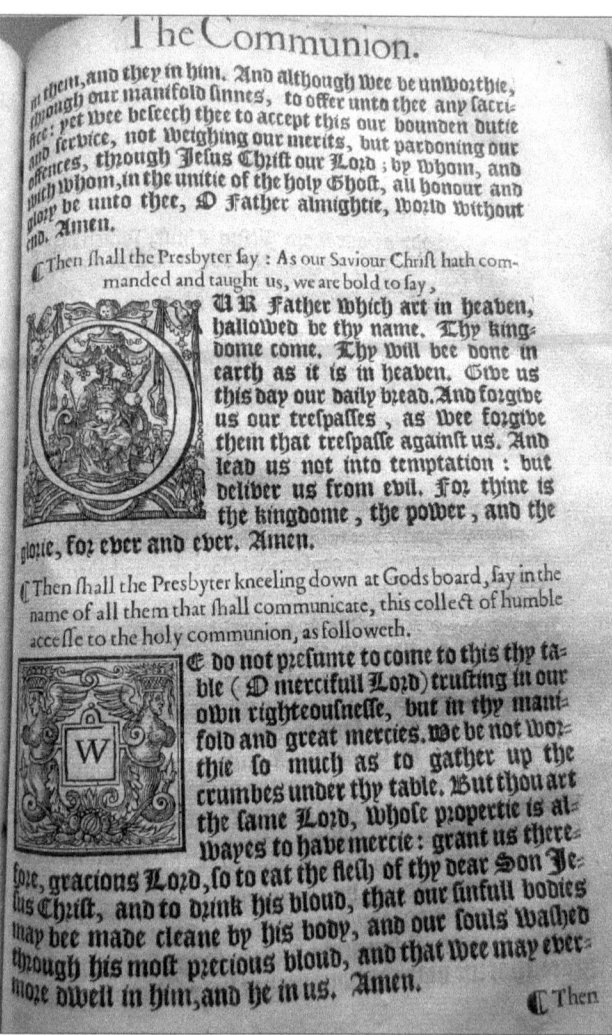

Plate 49. The Lord's Prayer and Prayer of Humble Access from the 1637 Scottish BCP.

---

iii Cuming, 1969, p. 141; Spinks, 2017, pp. 38–41.

receive Communion and that it was more difficult to remove the altar back to its place designated by the 1552 Book. They were also designed to keep stray animals out of the sanctuary. The practice in Elizabeth's reign had been to move the altar when it was to be used to the west end of the chancel or into the nave and position it so that the long sides were north and south.

The pattern of services continued much as they had been in Elizabeth's reign, with the metrical Psalms of Sternhold and Hopkins remaining unchallenged. In 1623, the Prayer Book was bound with the whole Bible and Apocrypha including 'The Genealogies recorded in the Holy Scriptures'.

CHARLES I AND THE SCOTTISH REVISION OF 1637

James died on Sunday, 27th March 1625. Charles I was crowned on 2nd February - Candlemas - 1626. There was no new Prayer Book under Charles but much controversy concerning the conduct and architectural setting of worship.

The Scottish Reformation had been formalised in 1560 when the Scottish Church broke with the Church of Rome. The 1560 Reformation Settlement that reformed the Church's doctrine and government was not recognised by the crown for some years. In 1572, the acts of 1560 were finally approved by the young James VI, but under pressure from the nobles, the Concordat of Leith also allowed the Crown to appoint bishops with the approval of the Church. In response to the new Concordat, a presbyterian party emerged headed by Andrew Melville.

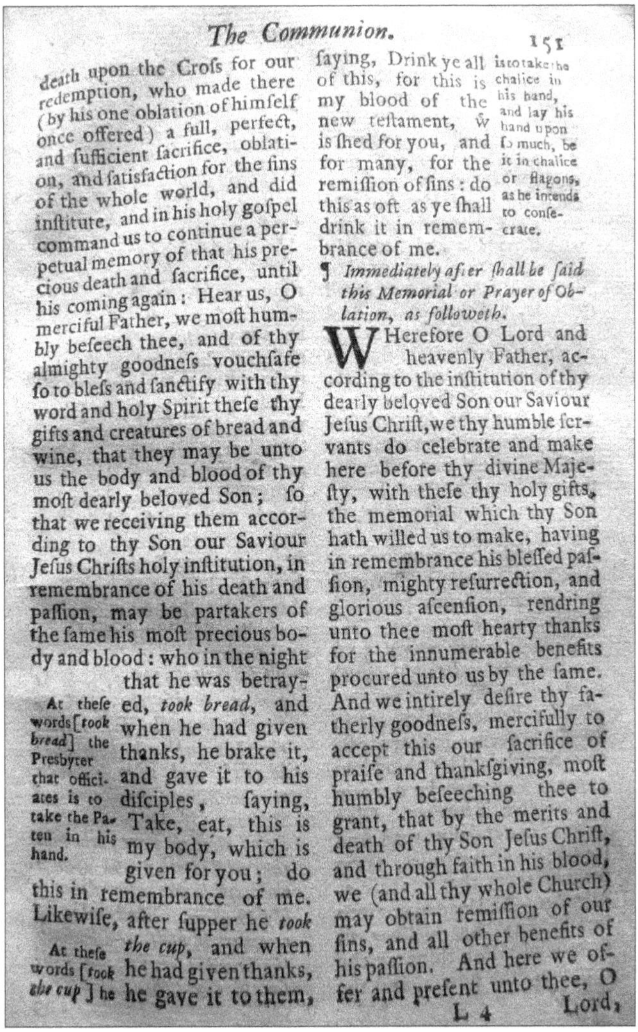

The Communion. 151

death upon the Crofs for our redemption, who made there (by his one oblation of himfelf once offered) a full, perfect, and fufficient facrifice, oblation, and fatisfaction for the fins of the whole world, and did inftitute, and in his holy gofpel command us to continue a perpetual memory of that his precious death and facrifice, until his coming again: Hear us, O merciful Father, we moft humbly befeech thee, and of thy almighty goodnefs vouchfafe fo to blefs and fanctify with thy word and holy Spirit thefe thy gifts and creatures of bread and wine, that they may be unto us the body and blood of thy moft dearly beloved Son; fo that we receiving them according to thy Son our Saviour Jefus Chrifts holy inftitution, in remembrance of his death and paffion, may be partakers of the fame his moft precious body and blood: who in the night that he was betrayed, *took bread*, and when he had given thanks, he brake it, and gave it to his difciples, faying, Take, eat, this is my body, which is given for you; do this in remembrance of me. Likewife, after fupper he *took the cup*, and when he had given thanks, he gave it to them, faying, Drink ye all of this, for this is my blood of the new teftament, ŵ is fhed for you, and for many, for the remiffion of fins: do this as oft as ye fhall drink it in remembrance of me.

At thefe words [*took bread*] the Presbyter that officiates is to take the Paten in his hand.

At thefe words [*took the cup*] he is to take the chalice in his hand, and lay his hand upon fo much, be it in chalice or flagons, as he intends to confecrate.

¶ *Immediately after fhall be faid this Memorial or Prayer of Oblation, as followeth.*

WHerefore O Lord and heavenly Father, according to the inftitution of thy dearly beloved Son our Saviour Jefus Chrift, we thy humble fervants do celebrate and make here before thy divine Majefty, with thefe thy holy gifts, the memorial which thy Son hath willed us to make, having in remembrance his bleffed paffion, mighty refurrection, and glorious afcenfion, rendring unto thee moft hearty thanks for the innumerable benefits procured unto us by the fame. And we intirely defire thy fatherly goodnefs, mercifully to accept this our facrifice of praife and thankfgiving, moft humbly befeeching thee to grant, that by the merits and death of thy Son Jefus Chrift, and through faith in his blood, we (and all thy whole Church) may obtain remiffion of our fins, and all other benefits of his paffion. And here we offer and prefent unto thee, O Lord,

L 4

Plate 50. Prayer of Consecration showing the reinstated epiclesis and Memorial or Prayer of Oblation with the reinstated anamnesis; from a Scottish BCP of 1637 printed in 1712 for the Rising of 1715. Once owned by Cameron of Locheil of Fessfern where Bonnie Prince Charlie slept a night after the rallying of the clans at Glenfinnan in 1745.

The Scottish Episcopal Church was formed as a distinct church in 1582 when the Church of Scotland rejected episcopal government and adopted a presbyterian government by elders and a General Assembly. However, from 1616, James I had been pushing the Scottish bishops towards a new Scottish Prayer Book. Charles I pursued his father's ambition. It was Laudian ideals that informed the Scottish bishops, and although the result became known as 'Laud's Liturgy', it was in fact the work of the Scottish bishops James Wedderburn and John Maxwell. In April 1636, the king approved the full manuscript, and printing was completed in 1637.

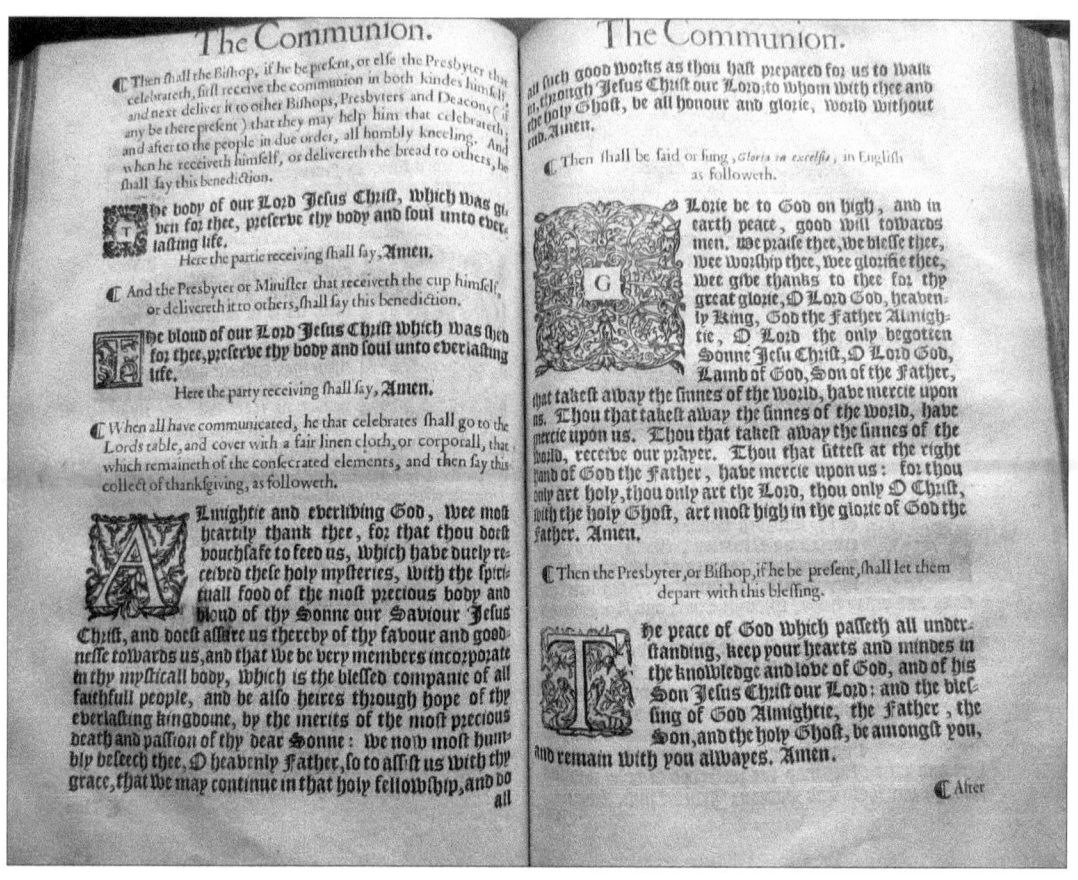

Plate 51. *The Words of Administration, Prayer of Thanksgiving, Gloria and Blessing from the 1637 Scottish BCP.*

The text, particularly of Holy Communion, owed much to the 1549 Prayer Book but with some Scottish concessions; for instance, presbyter was used instead of priest. The Institution Prayer, now named 'The Prayer of Consecration', restored the 1549 prayer of the Holy Spirit's blessing of the elements – the epiclesis – and this was followed by the 'Memorial or Prayer of Oblation'. This was succeeded by the Lord's Prayer and Prayer of Humble Access before the administration of Communion, which now used the words of 1549 without those of 1552 and concluded with the people's 'Amen'. They stressed that the bread and wine were in some way the Body and Blood of Christ. Any consecrated elements remaining were not to be taken from the church but consumed by 'such of the communicants only as the Presbyter which celebrated shall take unto him'. The holy table should stand at the time of Communion at the uppermost part of the chancel where the presbyter standing at the north end or side shall conduct the whole service. A reference to the departed was inserted into the prayer for the Church Militant. The option to sing the Creed was restored and regulations about further consecreation and consumption of the remaining consecrated elements was added.

The Scots felt the book reeked of popery and gave it a stormy reception. The protests that ensued were captured in popular imagination by the story of Jenny Geddes hurling a stool in protest in St Giles, Edinburgh, shouting, 'Villain! Do you say Mass at my lug?' Behind the folklore was a Presbyterian party strongly opposed to episcopacy in any form.

Although at the time of its introduction in Scotland in July 1637 it was soon rejected, it nevertheless influenced the English version of 1661/62 and, more importantly perhaps, proved a model for the Prayer Book of the Scottish Episcopal Church and thereby also the American Prayer Book of 1789, as well as that of the Province of South Africa in 1954 and the proposed English Book of 1928.

THE COMMONWEALTH AND THE SUPPRESSION OF THE BOOK OF COMMON PRAYER

Events proceeded apace with the 1638 National Covenant, ejection of episcopacy and the invasion of England, which contributed to the series of events leading to the English Civil War. The Puritans were in the ascendant, and they wanted more than just the revision of the Prayer Book. 'Root and branch' was their rallying cry, and it applied to Prayer Book and episcopacy alike. Bishop Cosin went into exile, Bishop Wren to the Tower, and Archbishop Laud was executed on 10th January 1645.

As the relationship between the king and Parliament became increasingly fraught, the bishops found themselves to be the targets of much of the unrest. Communion rails were destroyed in Suffolk, Essex and Buckinghamshire. At Hingham, in Norfolk, the minister prayed: 'Oh Lord, we have offended thee in wearing the surplice, in signing with the cross and using the ring in marriage.' For some, the Prayer Book itself became a target of attack. As Parliament and the army took control so the Church of England became a non-episcopal church operating a compromised system between Parliamentarianism and Independence. Eventually, Ordinances from Parliament ordered the removal of superstitious images, altars and crucifixes and forbade the use of organs.

In place of the House of Bishops, Parliament appointed an assembly of divines, the Westminster Assembly. It produced the **Westminster Confession** and catechism, being made up of some of the best minds in the Church of England. The presence of Independents who considered all set forms of worship against the word of God meant that they were unable to come up with anything other than a Directory, which gave an outline of a form of service with a summary of the themes and doctrines that might or might not be used by the minister.[iv]

In January 1645, the use of the *Book of Common Prayer* was declared illegal.

---

iv Spinks, 2017, pp. 74–75.

Chapter 5

THE 1662 REVISION AND SEVENTEENTH-CENTURY ADDITIONS

THE KING'S RETURN, THE SAVOY CONFERENCE, THE 1662 PRAYER BOOK

On 29th May 1660, Charles I's son Charles entered the country on his thirtieth birthday to be acclaimed the new king by popular consent. The Restoration restored both bishops and the *Book of Common Prayer*.

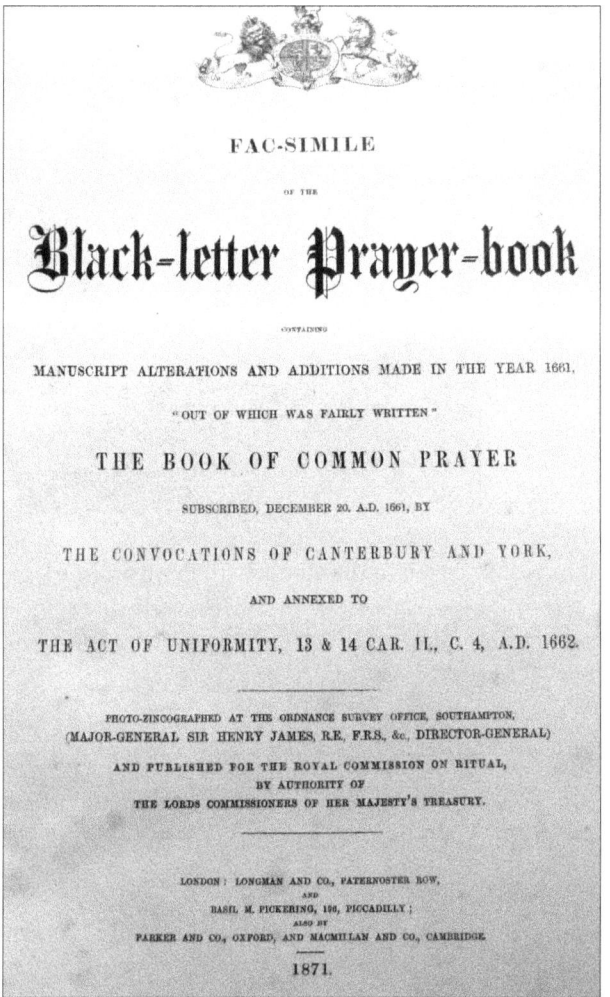

Plate 52. Title page of the 1871 Facsimile of the 1636 BCP used by Sancroft which became the Convocation copy.

Both high churchmen and the godly alike saw this as an opportunity to promote their own causes of reform to the text of the Prayer Book. Bishop Wren, promoted to the See of Ely, had spent eighteen years in the Tower of London contemplating its revision. His recommendations were published in a manuscript known as 'The Advices'. He advocated the removal of archaisms 'with as little alteration as well may be'.[i] John Cosin, later Bishop of Durham, who had spent seventeen years in exile in Paris, also produced his own suggestions, in all probability after seeing the Advices. Cosin and Wren combined their suggestions in an altered edition of the 1619 *Book of Common Prayer* compiled by Cosin, which became known as the **Durham Book**. It was Laudian in doctrine and relied heavily upon the Scottish Book of 1637.

---

i Cuming, 1969, p. 150.

Those of a strongly Reformed persuasion were led by Richard Baxter and Edward Reynolds, Bishop of Norwich. They produced ninety-six criticisms or **'Exceptions'** concerning general principles, defective wording and objectionable usage. These provided a comprehensive summary of the objections of the godly to the Prayer Book over the last century of controversy. One of their concerns was the presence of too much congregational participation in the services. Baxter produced a liturgy of his own.

On 25th March 1661, a Royal Warrant was issued establishing a commission to work on the revision of the Prayer Book and resolve these conflicting opinions. The Warrant authorised the Commissioners:

Plate 53. Title Page of the 1636 BCP with corrections in Sancroft's handwriting in an 1871 facsimile.

> to advise upon and review the said Book of Common Prayer, comparing the same with the most ancient liturgies which have been used in the Church, in the primitive and purest times…avoiding…all unnecessary alterations of the forms and liturgy wherewith the people are already acquainted, and have so long received within the Church of England.[ii]

It met in the Bishop of London's lodging in the Savoy Hospital and has been known ever since as the **Savoy Conference**. Among the Presbyterian party were its leaders, Edward Reynolds and Richard Baxter, who would decline the See of Hereford. The episcopal party was led by Gilbert Sheldon, Bishop of London, John Cosin, Bishop of Durham, Robert Sanderson and William Sancroft, who at the time was chaplain to John Cosin but was later to become archbishop. However, it was not liturgical scholars but politicians who managed the Conference, and they were in favour of making as few alterations to the Prayer Book as possible.

---

ii Cuming, 1969, p. 154.

The bishops announced that they were content with the Prayer Book and invited the godly to place their objections. They presented the Exceptions and Baxter's liturgy, but neither were accepted, being deemed to overstep the limits of the Royal Warrant. The bishops only conceded seventeen of their ninety-six points. The only one of significance was the acceptance of the Authorised Version of the Bible for all biblical readings, which did not affect the doctrine of the services. The gulf was too great between the differing sides, and the Conference broke up without agreement in July 1661. The work of revision now reverted to Convocation.

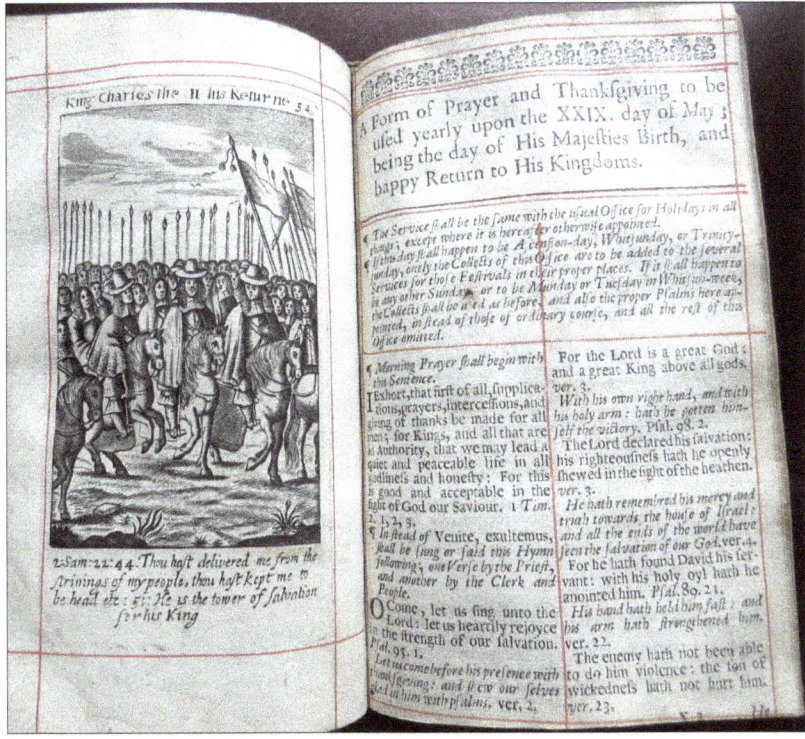

Plate 54. BCP 1680. State Service for the 29th May celebrating the Restoration and King Charles II's birthday.

Convocation had not been idle during the five months of the Conference and had drawn up an order of service for 29th May, to celebrate The Restoration, for 5th November and for 30th January for Charles the Martyr. These were later attached to the end of the Prayer Book and were known as **the State Services**. They remained part of the *Book of Common Prayer* until 1859 when they were rescinded by Royal Warrant. The bishops also produced a service of Baptism for those of riper years, made necessary by the disruption of the Commonwealth when many were not baptised as infants.

The bishops in Convocation worked from an amended copy of the Prayer Book compiled by William Sancroft on Bishop Cosin's bequest, which incorporated elements of the Durham Book and the Exceptions and which became known as the Fair Copy. Convocation's own recommendations were published in what became known as the **'Convocation Book'**, and this was attached to the Act on Uniformity, being known as the 'Annexed Book'. In 1871, a facsimile copy of the Convocation Book, a corrected copy of the Black-letter Prayer Book of 1636 with Sancroft's handwritten notes in the margin, was published, an edition of which remains in the collection. When the final copy was given the Royal Assent under the Great Seal, it became the **Sealed Copy**. The new Act of Uniformity, which had received Royal Assent on 19th May 1662, provided that by 24th August, St Bartholomew's Day, every licensed dignitary, fellow, incumbent, curate, and teacher within the Church of England should have read Morning and Evening Prayer and made public declaration of his unfeigned assent and consent to all that it contained.[iii]

Compared with the earlier revisions of 1559 and 1604, this was more thorough. The language was updated, new services included and rubrics were amended. The wording of the title page was expanded. Two Acts of Uniformity, that of Elizabeth I and Charles II, were included. A new Preface was written, probably by Sanderson, which nevertheless relied heavily upon earlier ones and was intended to commend the Book for universal approval:

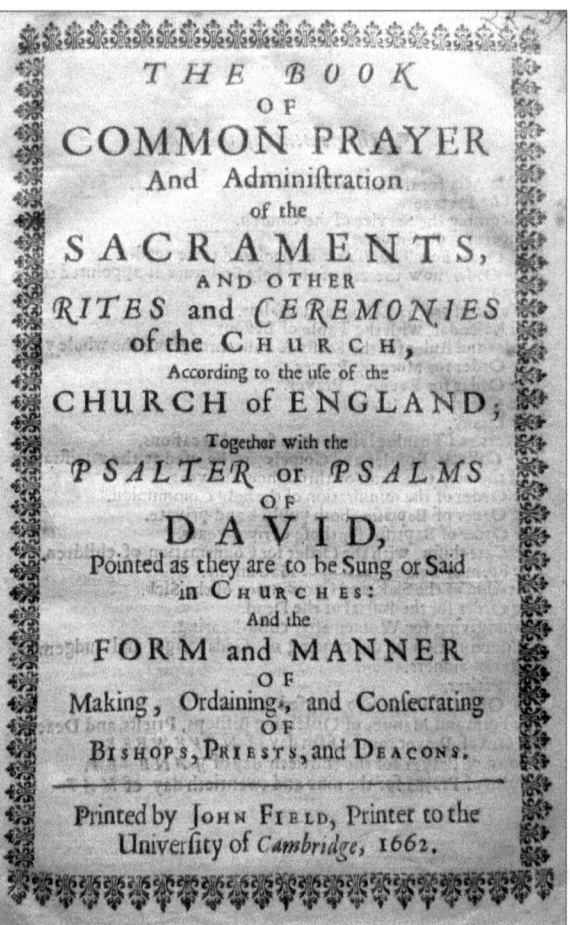

Plate 55. Title page of the new 1662 BCP with expanded wording.

> It had been the wisdom of the Church of England, ever since the compiling of her Public Liturgy, to keep the mean between the two extremes, of too much stiffness in refusing and too much easiness in admitting any variation from it...Our general aim...was...to do that, which is to our best understanding we conceive might most tend to the preservation of Peace and Unity in the Church; the procuring of reverence and the exciting of Piety and Devotion in the Public Worship of God...

Prayers for the King and Royal Family were added to Morning and Evening Prayer and were also included in the Litany. The Athanasian Creed was taken out of Evening Prayer and printed separately afterwards. A new section of Prayers and Thanksgivings after the Litany included The **General Thanksgiving**, written originally by Bishop Reynolds for the Directory, also a Prayer for All Conditions of Men, probably written by Reynolds. There are also prayers for rain, fair weather, plenty, peace and

---

iii Griffiths, 2002, p. 108.

deliverance from enemies, restoring public peace at home (written by Bishop Wren) and for deliverance from the plague 'and other common sicknesses'. New Collects, Epistles and Gospels were provided for St Stephen's Day, Innocents Day, and Epiphany Six, proper Psalms for Ash Wednesday and Good Friday, an extra Easter Anthem and a Collect for Easter Even. The Epistles and Gospel readings were to be read from the 1611 Bible.

The final rubric of Holy Communion was taken from the 1637 Book and required unused elements to be consumed by the priest or someone appointed by him. The motive for this rubric was to avoid the appearance of irreverence rather than any theological reason. The **Black Rubric**, which had been omitted in 1559 and 1603, was now restored but with a significant change of wording. In 1552, the rubric repudiated belief in the 'real and essential presence' in the elements of bread and wine. Now the rubric repudiated the 'corporal'

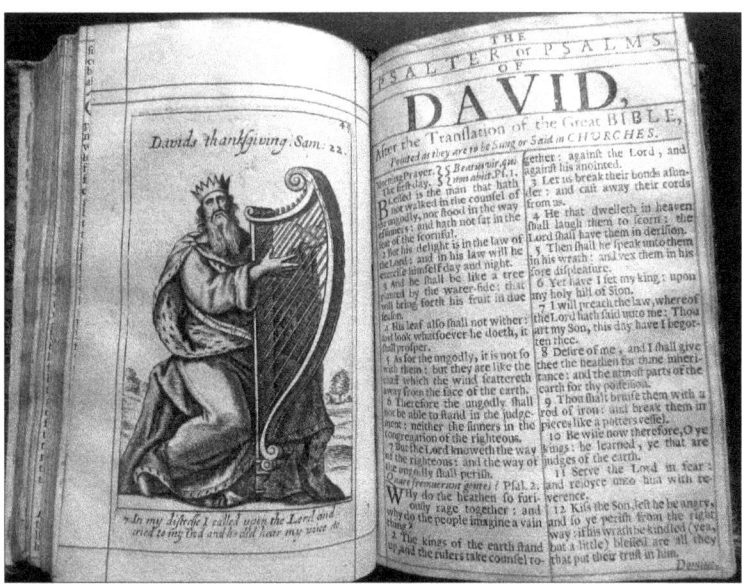

Plate 56. 1680 BCP. The Psalms of David were taken from the Great Bible in 1662.

(i.e. physical) presence. Since the seventeenth century, many divines did believe in the 'real and essential presence', or sacramental presence.[iv] The Words of Institution were now called the Prayer of Consecration, although there was no epiclesis or request for consecration. However, manual acts were restored during the Words of Institution so that the Fraction took place during the prayer. Also restored were the offering of the elements (without words of oblation), thanksgiving for the faithful departed and permission to sing the Creed and *Sanctus*.

> The essential fact about consecration in the English service is that it is a prayer...[It] is not an explicit prayer for the consecration of the elements, which is its essential difference from 1549, but a prayer for the gift of the heavenly realities to those who receive...The Prayer Book properly understood, has therefore no 'moment of consecration'...There is an all-important difference between offering a sacrifice and pleading a sacrifice...We cannot offer Christ, but we must be united with him

---

iv Spinks, 2017, p. 87.

in his death and resurrection and offer ourselves 'in and through him'. The whole Consecration Prayer therefore 'proclaims the Lord's death until he comes'...There is no point in asserting that the English Consecration Prayer is perfect...but its intention is perfectly clear, and that intention it achieves.[v]

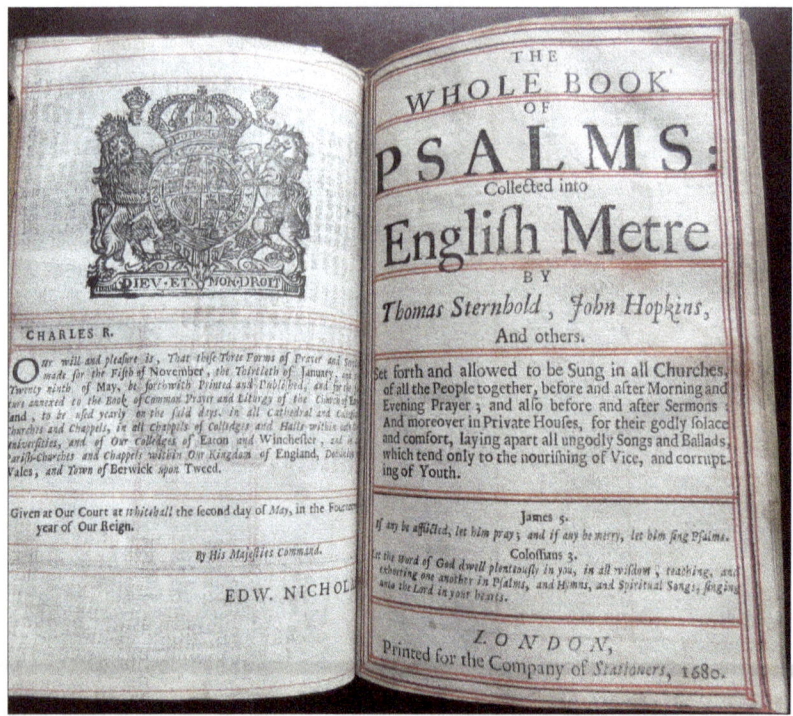

Plate 57. 1680 BCP. The Whole Book of Psalms in English Metre by Thomas Sternhold and John Hopkins with the authorisation of William III and Queen Mary.

A prayer explicitly blessing the water is added to the Baptismal rite. The Psalter was formally included in the 1662 Book and followed Coverdale's text of the Great Bible.

A new Office, 'The Order of Prayers to be Used at Sea', was expanded from prayers compiled for the Directory of 1644 for sailors who were found to be using the discontinued Prayer Book.

The Ordinal was now formally incorporated into the Prayer Book. It now made clear that bishops constituted a separate ordering and were not merely priests 'consecrated' or appointed to that office, dispelling the Puritan notion of the parity of all ministers. The priesthood is also defined as dependent upon episcopal ordination. Cosin's version of 'Come Holy Ghost' from his 'Devotions' replaced the rather poor hymn that Cranmer had provided at ordinations.[vi]

When the Act of Uniformity was passed in 1662, an unintended consequence was the departure of approximately two thousand ministers from the Church of England who refused to swear the oath of loyalty to the use of the Prayer Book and were ejected from their livings in what came to be known as the Great Ejection, so creating Dissent and Nonconformity.

---

v Harrison, 1959, pp. 67–69.

vi Harrison, 1959, p. 87.

SUPPLEMENTARY SECTIONS TO THE BOOK OF COMMON PRAYER

From time to time, additions were made to the *Book of Common Prayer* that were not included in the list of contents. In several editions from 1679 to 1683, there appeared 'A Form of Prayer...to be Used on the 2nd of September for the Dreadful Fire of London' that had occurred in 1666.

An early form of the Accession Service was 'The King's Day' service, which first appeared in the reign of James II (1685–1688). A formal Prayer Book Accession Service has been in use since the reign of Queen Anne. In 1816, it was called 'The King's Accession', and in 1901, it was simplified so that fewer emendations would be needed at each accession.[vii]

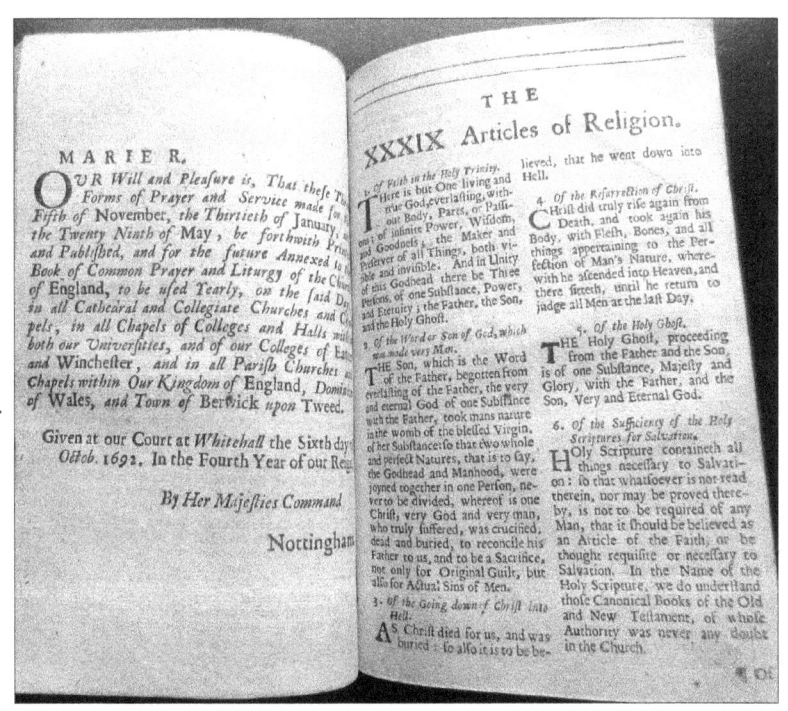

Plate 58. 1694 BCP. The 39 Articles of Religion authorised for inclusion by Queen Mary.

The Thirty-Nine Articles appeared in the *Book of Common Prayer* in 1682 and were included frequently thereafter. The Table of Kindred and Affinity was compiled by Archbishop Parker in 1503 and first appeared in the Prayer Book in 1681. It has featured regularly since that time.

'CONSTITUTIONS AND CANONS ECCLESIASTICAL for the PROVINCE OF CANTERBURY agreed upon with the KING'S MAJESTIES licence...1603...and in the year of the reign of our SOVEREIGN LORD JAMES...KING OF ENGLAND, FRANCE AND IRELAND THE FIRST and of SCOTLAND the thirty-seventh' first appeared in the Prayer Book of 1682 and occasionally in folio editions thereafter.

The service 'At the Healing' went back to the time of Edward the Confessor. Sufferers from scrofula were brought to the monarch for the laying-on-of-hands apparently

---

vii Griffiths, 2002, p. 111.

popular in the reign of Queen Anne and only printed in the Prayer Book between 1704 and 1732.

A regular feature of the seventeenth-century Prayer Book was the Metrical Psalms. The 'old version' of Thomas Sternhold and John Hopkins was widely used from 1549 to 1696 but only occasionally after that, although in some instances, both the 'old' and the 'new' versions were included. On 3rd December 1696, William III gave approval to 'A New Version of the Psalms of David...' written by N. Brady and N. Tate. These were bound with the Prayer Book until the middle of the nineteenth century.[viii]

The alterations in the *Book of Common Prayer* authorised in 1662, though many, were not substantial. Essentially, it was the 1552 Book with updated language, rubrics which encouraged more high church practice and some excellent prayers written by Protestant Divines. Gilbert Sheldon's sense of the English man's and woman's appreciation of the Prayer Book being a moderate churchman himself was more in tune with the nation's temper than the opinions of either John Cosin or Richard Baxter.

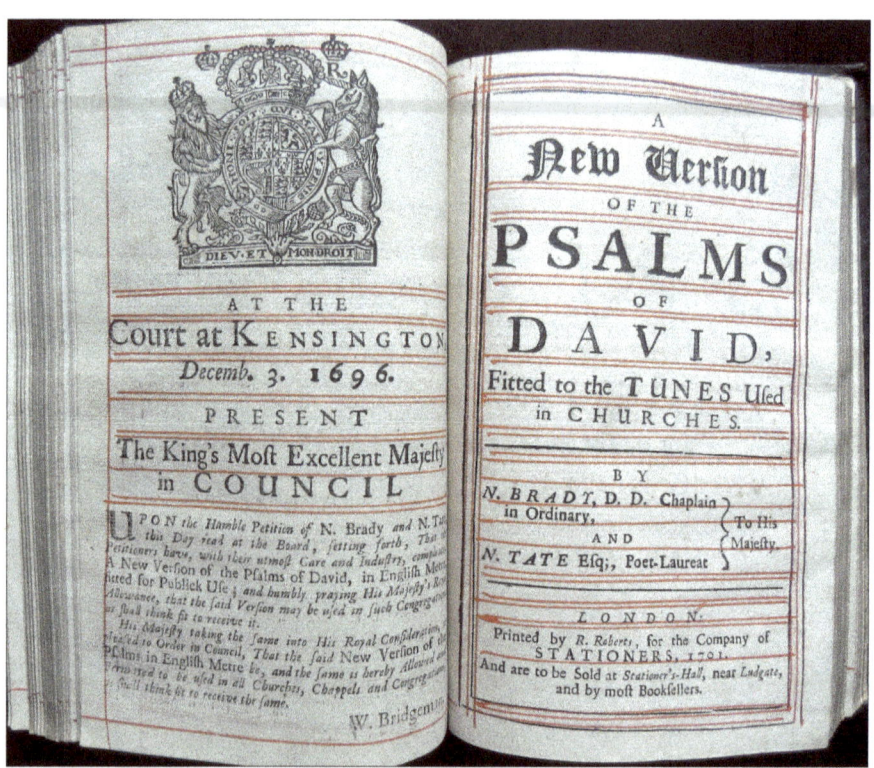

Plate 59. 1704 BCP. 'New' Metrical Psalms by N. Brady and N. Tate authorised by the King in Council.

---

viii Griffiths, 2002, p. 112.

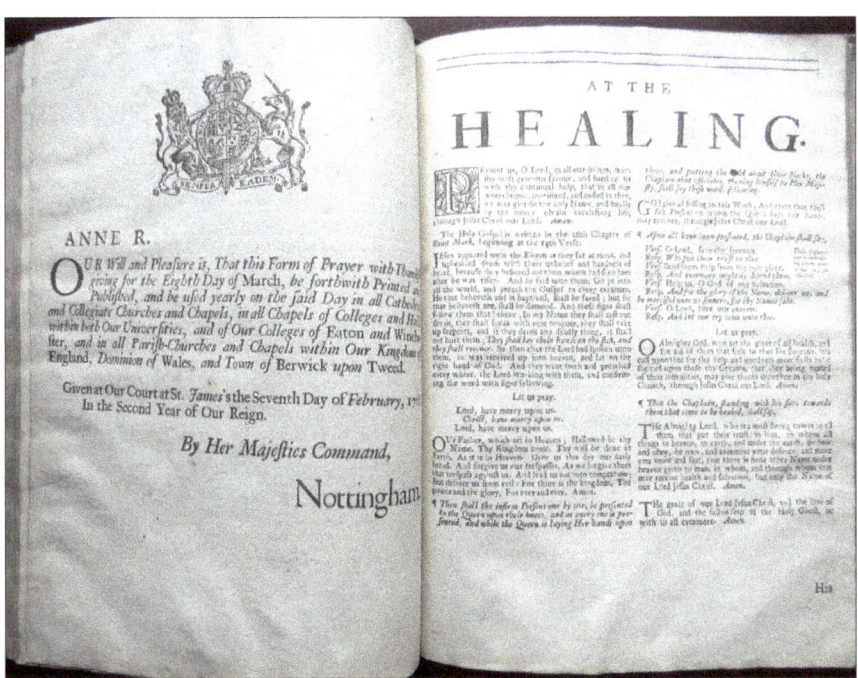

Plate 60. 1704 BCP. The service 'At the Healing', authorised by Queen Anne.

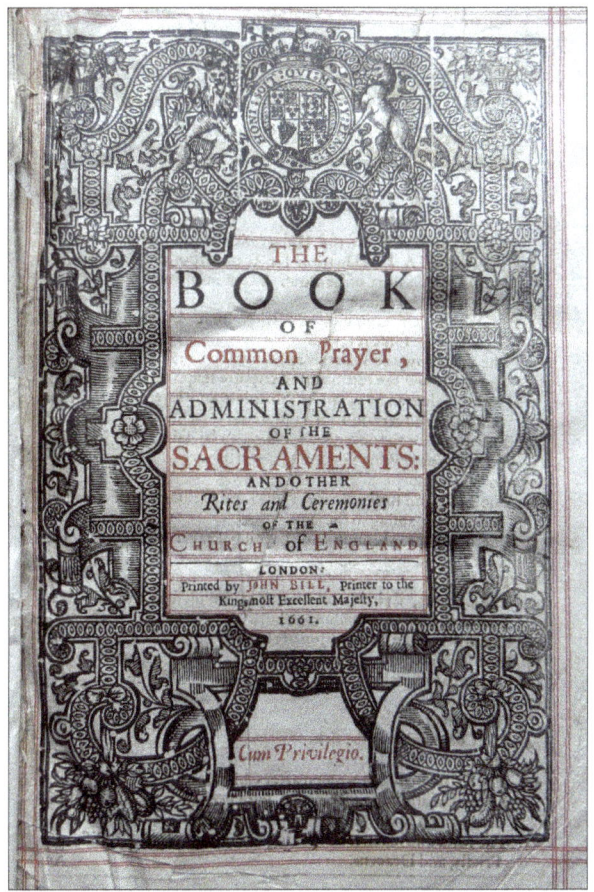

Plate 61. Title page of the 1661 BCP, printed by John Bill.

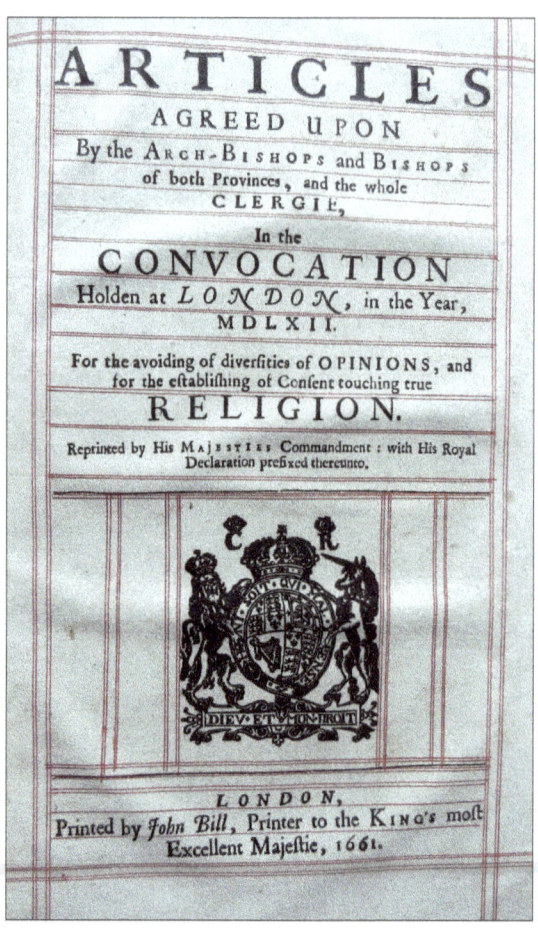

Plate 62 1661 BCP. Articles of Religion title page.

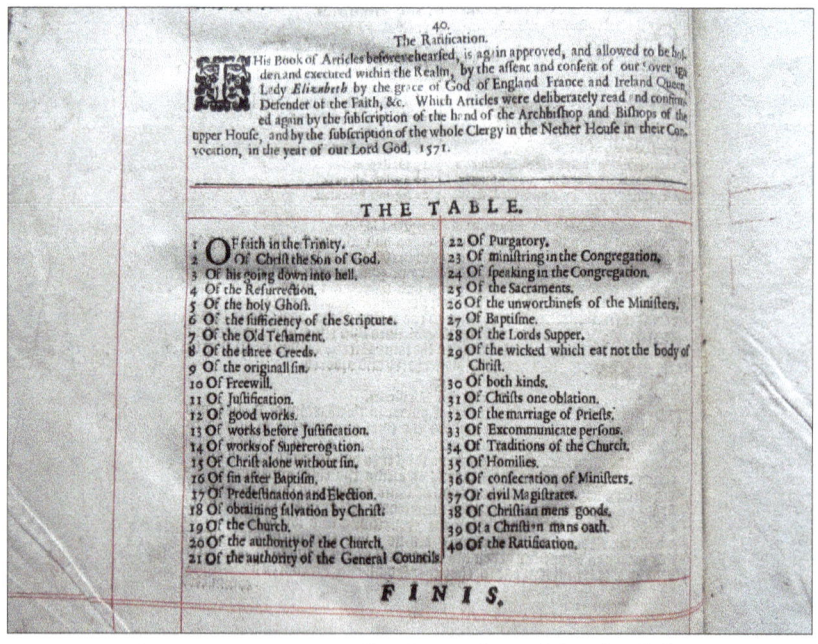

Plate 63. 1661 BCP. Ratification of the Articles of Religion which were first drawn up in 1571.

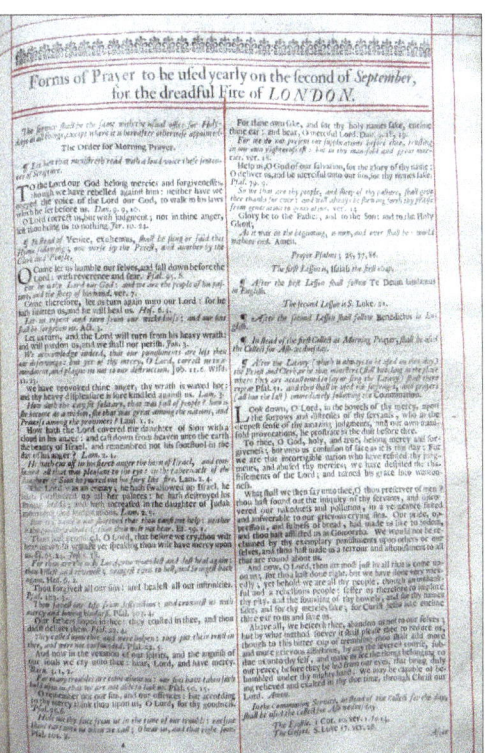

Plate 64. 1683 BCP. Form of Prayer to be used on the 2nd September for the dreadful Fire of London.

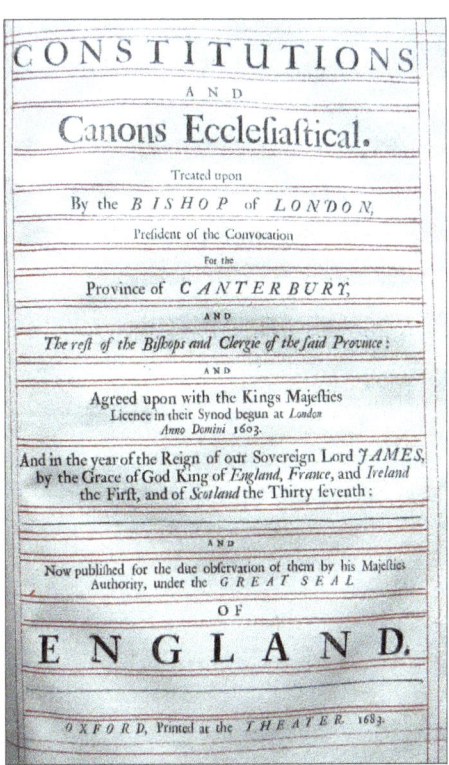

Plate 65. 1683 BCP. Constitutions and Canons Ecclesiastical...of England.

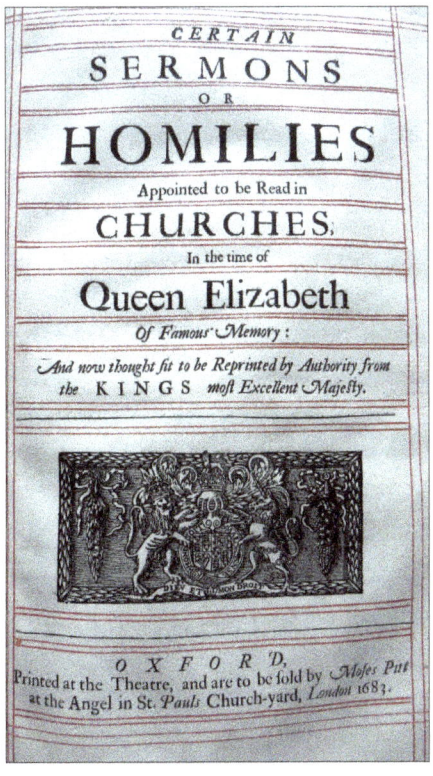

Plate 66. 1683 BCP. Sermons and Homilies from E 1.

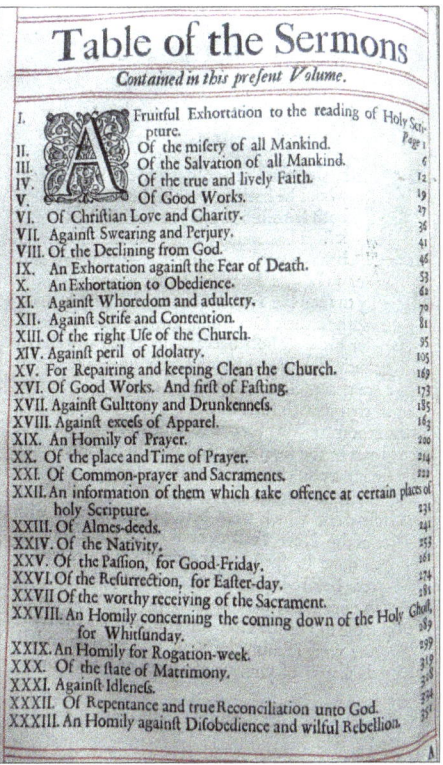

Plate 67. 1683 BCP. The Table of Sermons.

APPENDIX 3

1552 BCP	1637 BCP	1662 BCP
THE ORDER	The Lord's Prayer	The Lord's Prayer
Collect for Purity	Collect for Purity	Collect for Purity
Ten Commandments	Ten Commandments	Ten Commandments
Collect of the Day	One of two Collects for the King	One of two Collects for the King
One of two Collects for the King	Collect of the Day	Collect of the Day
Epistle	Epistle	Epistle
Gospel	Gospel	Gospel
Nicene Creed	Nicene Creed	Nicene Creed
Sermon or homily or Exhortation (as set)	Sermon or homily or Exhortation (as set)	Notices and offertory sentence
Notices and offertory sentence	Notices and offertory sentence	Sermon or homily or Exhortation (as set)
The collection	The collection	The collection
Prayer for the whole estate of Christ's Church	Prayer for the whole estate of Christ's Church	Prayer for the whole estate of Christ's Church
Exhortation to regular Communion	Exhortation to regular Communion	(additional Exhortation at the priest's discretion)
(additional Exhortation at the priest's discretion)	(additional Exhortation at the priest's discretion)	Exhortation to regular Communion
Exhortation to come to Communion worthily	Exhortation to come to Communion worthily	Exhortation to come to Communion worthily
Invitation to confession	Invitation to confession	Invitation to confession
General confession	General confession	General confession
Absolution	Absolution	Absolution
Comfortable Words	Comfortable Words	Comfortable Words
Sursum Corda	Sursum Corda	Sursum Corda
Proper Preface	Proper Preface	Proper Preface
'Therefore with angels...'	'Therefore with angels...'	'Therefore with angels...'
Prayer of Humble Access	Prayer of Consecration (with epiclesis)	Prayer of Humble Access
Prayer of Consecration (without epiclesis)	Prayer of Oblation; 'mercifully to accept this our sacrifice of praise and thanksgiving...'	Prayer of Consecration (without epiclesis)
Priest and people receive Communion: 'Take and eat this in remembrance that Christ died for thee, and feed on him in thy heart by faith with thanksgiving.'	Lord's Prayer with the people repeating after the priest.	Priest and people receive Communion: (words of 1549 and 1552 combined)
Lord's Prayer with the people repeating after the priest.	Prayer of Humble Access	Lord's Prayer with the people repeating after the priest.
Prayer of Oblation; 'mercifully to accept this our sacrifice of praise and thanksgiving...' OR	Priest and people receive Communion: 'The body of our Lord Jesus Christ which was given for thee, preserve thy body and soul unto everlasting life.' (1549)	Prayer of Oblation; 'mercifully to accept this our sacrifice of praise and thanksgiving...' OR
Prayer of Thanksgiving	Prayer of Thanksgiving	Prayer of Thanksgiving
Gloria	Gloria	Gloria
Blessing by priest or bishop.	Blessing by priest or bishop.	Blessing by priest or bishop.

Chapter 6

THE NON-JURORS AND THE PRAYER BOOK IN THE EIGHTEENTH CENTURY

THE NON-JURORS PRAYER BOOK

One of the most interesting and rare editions in Humphrey Paine's collection is the Non-Jurors' Prayer Book of 1718. Who were the Non-Jurors and of what did their Prayer Book consist?

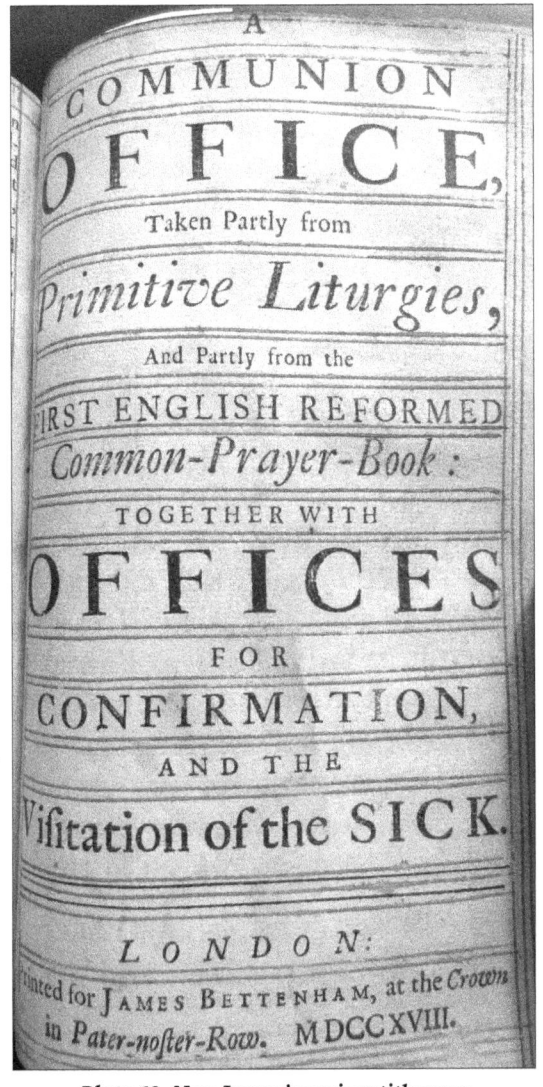

Plate 68. Non-Jurors' services title page in the BCP of 1727.

When Charles II died in 1685, he left the throne to his Catholic brother James. James wished to make life easier for his Catholic co-religionists with particular reference to their ability to hold teaching posts in the universities and issued, what in America would be called an Executive Order, a Declaration of Indulgence. This caused alarm in political circles, and to curry favour with another group, James tried to extend toleration to Dissenters as well. However, due to the illegality of James' Declaration, seven bishops refused to announce it from the pulpit and were not only deprived of their sees but placed in the Tower. They were regarded as public heroes, and such was the political fallout that when, on the invitation of leading Tories, James' sister Mary and her Dutch husband William landed at Torbay in Devon in November 1688 with an armed escort, he fled the country.

William and Mary were declared to hold the throne jointly. However, the irony of the situation was that some of the same high churchmen who, out of conscience, had been unable to support James' illegal Declaration now felt themselves unable to swear allegiance to William and Mary while James was still alive because of their high regard for the Divine Right of Kings and loyalty to the Established Church. William Sancroft, now Archbishop, together with Bishops Turner of Ely, Lake of Chichester, Thomas of Worcester, White of Peterborough, Ken of Bath and Wells (well-known as a hymn writer), Lloyd of Norwich and Frampton of Gloucester were deprived of their sees as well as some four hundred parish clergy who lost their livings and were prepared to accept obscurity and poverty. They became known as the Non-Jurors. Many fled to Scotland where the Nonjuring Scottish bishops welcomed their colleagues' liturgy.

A personal twist to the story is that Humphrey Paine's final post was that of the parishes of Fressingfield and Weybread in the St Edmundsbury diocese on the Norfolk/Suffolk border, the very place where Archbishop Sancroft lived out his final days.

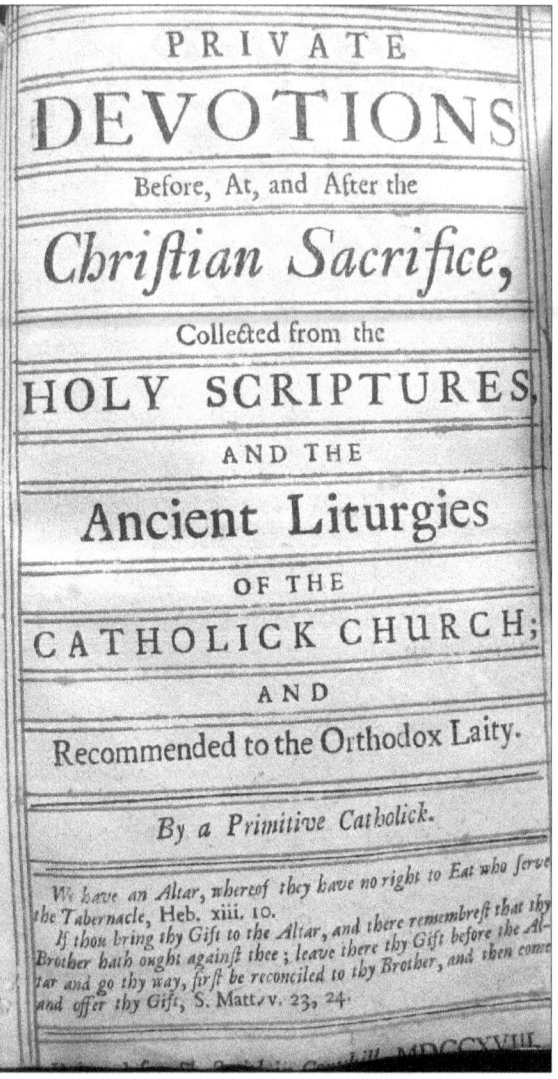

The Non-Jurors were divided between those whose main concern was the oath of allegiance and those passionate about a more primitive and authentic form of Eucharistic worship. The latter group became known as the Usagers and championed four 'uses' in particular: that water should be mixed with wine at the Communion, the inclusion of the epiclesis or invocation of the Holy Spirit upon the bread and wine, that the Prayer of Oblation be in the main canon of the Eucharist, and prayers for the departed included in the Prayer for the Church. Their model was the first Reformed Book of Edward VI, that of 1549, which they reprinted in 1717. The following year, 1718, they printed their own Book. The edition in Paine's collection is a Prayer Book of 1727, printed by John Baskett, in which all the services after the Readings have

Plate 69. Private Devotions before the Eucharist in the Non-Jurors' Prayer Book of 1718.

66   PETER S. PAINE: THE PRAYER BOOK REVEALED

been replaced by the Non-Juror's revised services of Holy Communion, Confirmation and Visitation of the Sick together with a section titled: 'Private Devotions before, at and after the Christian Sacrifice, collected from the Holy Scriptures and the Liturgies of the Catholic Church and Recommended to the Orthodox Laity, by a Primitive Catholic'. Their revised services were printed by James Bettenham at the Crown in Paternoster Row in 1718.

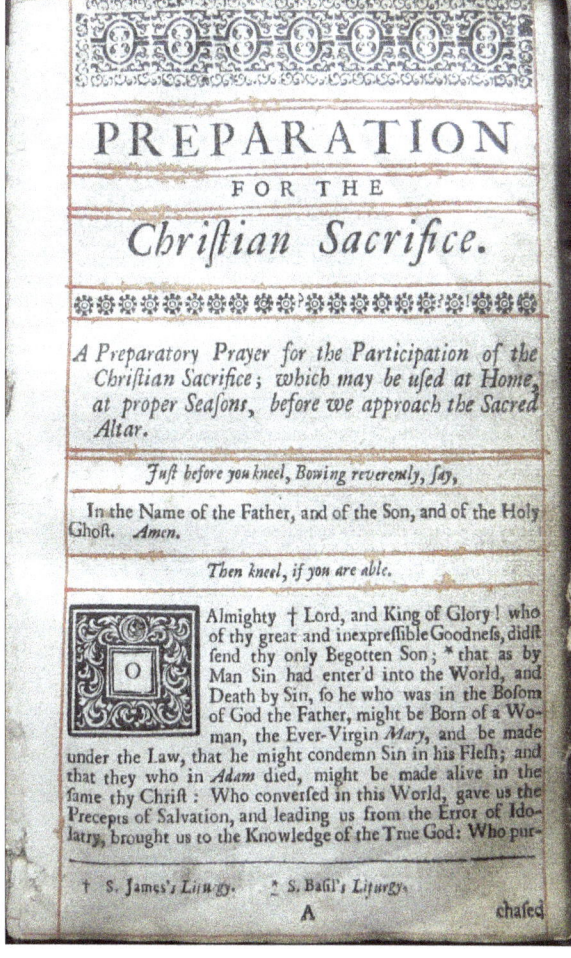

Plate 70. BCP 1727. Prayer of Preparation before Communion in Non-Jurors' Prayer Book with Patristic references.

The Preface to the service of **Holy Communion** and the other two services declares that 'the Eucharistic Sacrifice being the most efficacious means of pardon and grace, ought to be performed with proportionate Care and Solemnity'. It claims the rite to be based on 'Apostolic Precedent and Tradition' which, being the earliest record, was 'most...blessed with the Effusions of the Holy Spirit'.

When the elements have been placed upon the altar and before the *Sursum Corda*, the priest prays a prayer adapted from the *Liturgy of St Basil* that the ministers may be worthy to offer 'this reasonable and unbloody sacrifice' and that the grace of the Holy Spirit be sent down upon them. After the *Sanctus*, the Consecration Prayer begins with a paraphrase from the *Liturgy of St James*. Here, the reason why the Father sent his only begotten Son is to 'satisfy thy Justice, to strengthen our nature and remedy thine image within us', and Calvary is called 'the Propitiatory Sacrifice upon the cross'. The Prayer of Oblation that follows the Words of Institution is adapted from the *Apostolic Constitutions* 'for completing the Sacrifice and giving it the highest degree of Consecration'. The prayer begins with a full anamnesis and epiclesis in which the Holy Spirit is called down upon 'this Sacrifice, that he may make this Bread the Body of thy Christ; and this Cup the Blood of thy Christ; that they who are partakers thereof, may be confirmed in godliness...'.

The order of the prayers in the canon is that of the 1549 Book as are the words of the Prayer for the Whole State of Christ's Church, the Introits and Psalms. Three reasons for the omission of the Ten Commandments are given, and Christ's summary of the Law is substituted for them. The rest of the office is that 'of the English Liturgies' with the *Gloria* at the end as in 1552.

In the **Office of Confirmation**, the signing with the cross and Chrism are restored because 'they are no less significant here than in Baptism'. The cross was used in the first reformed liturgy and Chrism 'is an Emblem of Spiritual Unction...as it has been practiced in the Primitive and Universal Church'.

'The Anointing with Oil in the **Office for the Sick** is not only supported by Primitive Practice, but commanded by the Apostle *St James*. It is not here administered by way of *Extreme Unction*, but in order to Recovery.' This was a significant departure from what had come to be normal medieval practice. Anointing with oil was preceded by a prayer of blessing upon the oil that God might 'bless and sanctify this thy creature of oil...: Grant that those who shall be anointed therewith may be delivered from all pains, troubles

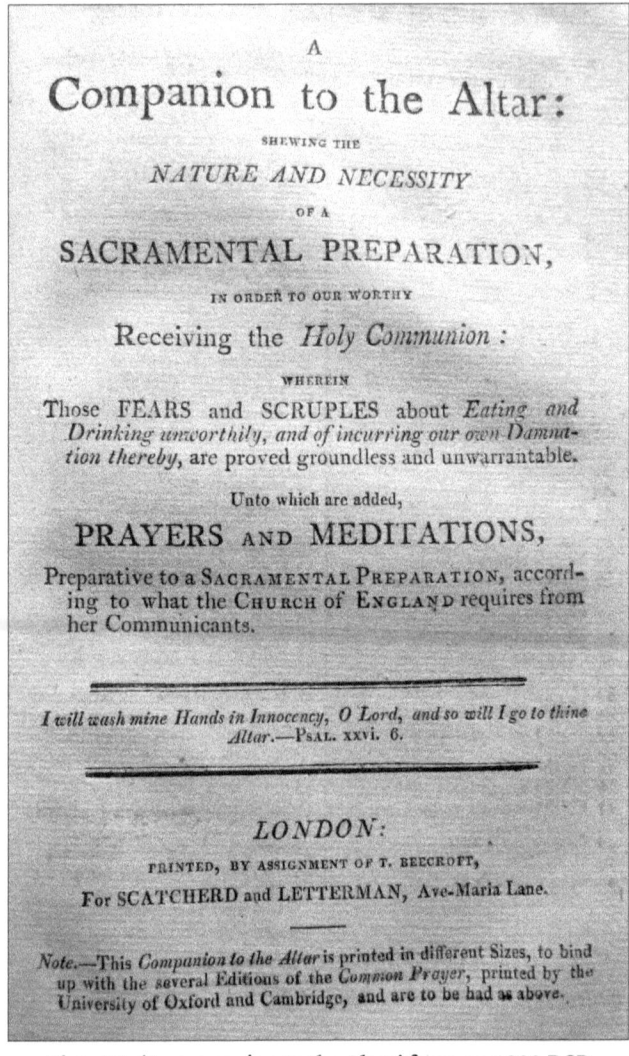

Plate 71. 'A companion to the Altar' from an 1803 BCP.

and diseases, both of body and mind...'. This consecration prayer is not to be used again until all the oil is spent. The sick person is then anointed with the oil on the forehead, making the sign of the Cross. The priest prays that through this outward sign of anointing, 'thy soul inwardly may be anointed with the Holy Ghost...'. The rite concludes with the Aaronic blessing. Additional prayers are provided for a sick child, a sick person at the point of departure and for a person troubled in mind or in conscience.

The Preface concludes:

> Upon the whole, here is nothing introduced without unexceptionable Warrant; nothing of late beginning: Here is no Application to Saints or Angels, no worship of Images, no Praying the Dead out of *Purgatory*, no Adoration of the Consecrated Elements; nothing that supposes a Corporal Presence, either by *Trans* or *Consubstantiation*; In short, nothing but what is Primitive and agreeable to Scripture, and practiced by the best recommended and enlightened ages.

All of which may be true but the fifteenth- and sixteenth-century Reformers including Cranmer would not have considered it sufficiently reformed while it commended a Patristic understanding of the Eucharist as a sacrifice.

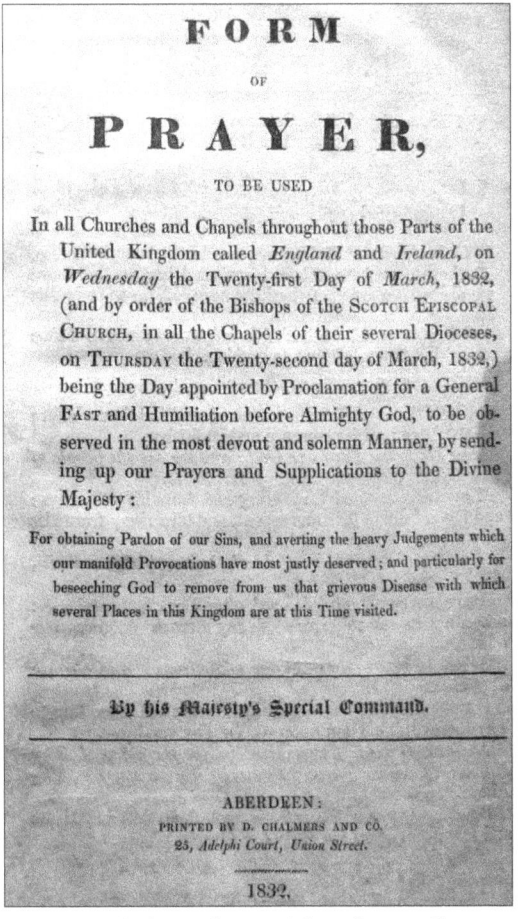

Plate 72. 'A form of Prayer' for grievous disease from an 1824 BCP.

Although this Non-Juror's Prayer Book was used only by the 'Usagers' and given that the Non-Jurors themselves were a dying breed, it may seem surprising to the reader that so much space has been given to a book very few people used. The reason is that its historical influence was significant.

After the death of Archbishop Sancroft and two others of the Nonjuring bishops, a decision was made to continue the line of succession, and with the permission of the exiled James II, two further bishops were consecrated. One of them, George Hickes, arranged with the Scottish bishops Archibald Cambell and James Gadderar to continue the English Nonjuring succession. The Scottish Episcopal bishops ejected from the Church of Scotland by the Presbyterians in 1689 also refused to take the oath to King William, and so the Scottish Episcopal Church, including those loyal to their bishops, was for a time a Nonjuring Church. With the death of Charles Edward Stuart in 1788, the Scottish bishops agreed to submit to the government of George II and they ceased to be a Nonjuring Church. The Scottish Episcopal Church became an independent Anglican Church using its own Communion Office based on that of 1637. The significance of this status and the influence of its liturgy will become apparent in a later chapter.

OCCASIONAL ADDITIONS TO THE PRAYER BOOK IN THE EIGHTEENTH AND NINETEENTH CENTURIES

Those who agreed the additions and alterations to the Prayer Book authorised in 1662 would have been amazed that it not only survived the Glorious Revolution of 1688/9 but was used with very little alteration for nearly three hundred years. During the following two centuries, there were several additional forms of service. A thanksgiving for the harvest, to be said after the General Thanksgiving, first appeared in 1796 and continued to be re-issued until 1847.[i]

There have been added to the services of the Prayer Book occasional forms of prayer promulgated in a few cases by Act of Parliament but generally by Royal Proclamation under the authority assumed to have been given the Crown by Section 26 of the Act of Uniformity of 1559, or under the authority of the Sovereign as the Supreme Head of the Church.[ii] A service for the occasion of the Great Fire of London in 1666 has already been noted as appearing in a 1683 edition of the Prayer Book. In 1784, the independence of the United States was acknowledged, as was Nelson's victory over the French at the Battle of the Nile in 1798 and Wellington's victory at Waterloo in 1815. In 1859, prayers were said for the suppression of the rebellion in Her Majesty's Indian Dominions; in 1866, during the prevalence of cholera and of cattle plague; and in 1877, for fifty years of Her Majesty's reign.

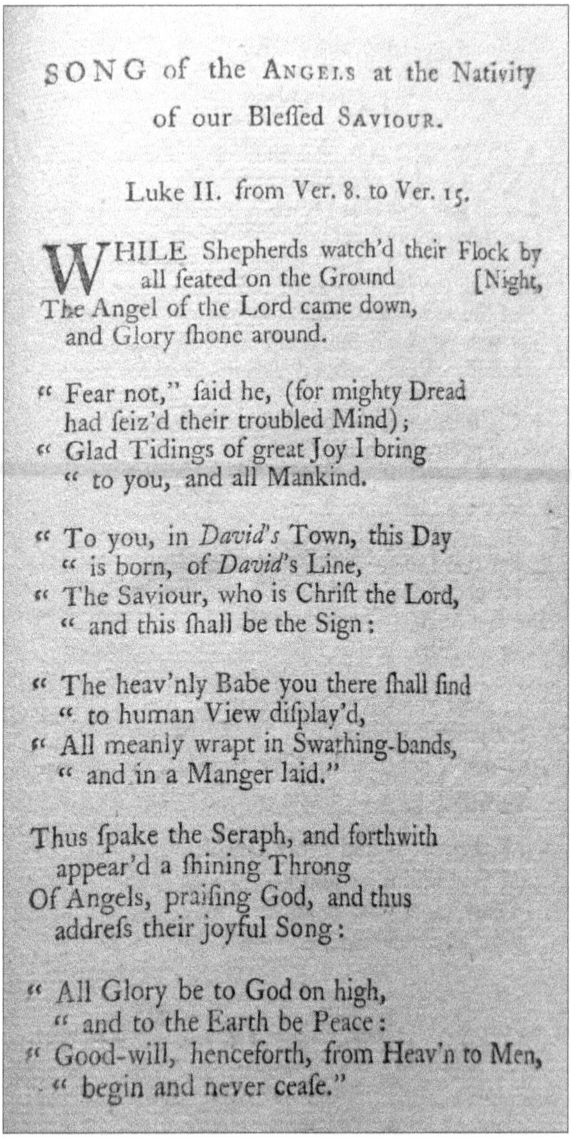
SONG of the ANGELS at the Nativity of our Bleſſed SAVIOUR.

Luke II. from Ver. 8. to Ver. 15.

WHILE Shepherds watch'd their Flock by all ſeated on the Ground [Night,
The Angel of the Lord came down,
and Glory ſhone around.

" Fear not," ſaid he, (for mighty Dread
had ſeiz'd their troubled Mind);
" Glad Tidings of great Joy I bring
" to you, and all Mankind.

" To you, in *David's* Town, this Day
" is born, of *David*'s Line,
" The Saviour, who is Chriſt the Lord,
" and this ſhall be the Sign:

" The heav'nly Babe you there ſhall find
" to human View diſplay'd,
" All meanly wrapt in Swathing-bands,
" and in a Manger laid."

Thus ſpake the Seraph, and forthwith
appear'd a ſhining Throng
Of Angels, praiſing God, and thus
addreſs their joyful Song:

" All Glory be to God on high,
" and to the Earth be Peace:
" Good-will, henceforth, from Heav'n to Men,
" begin and never ceaſe."

Plate 73. Christmas Hymn from a 1795 BCP.

A popular occasional addition to the Prayer Book was 'A Companion to the Altar', a preparation for Holy

i Cuming, 1969, p. 169.

ii Benton, 1910, p. xxxvii.

Communion consisting of 'Prayers and Meditations'. In 1832, there appeared 'A Form of Prayer to be used...on the 21st Day of March...for a General Fast and Humiliation before Almighty God...for obtaining pardon for our sins... and particularly for beseeching God to remove from us that grievous Disease with which several Places in this Kingdom are at this Time visited.' The specific 'disease' is not mentioned, but it could have been one of the two referred to above.

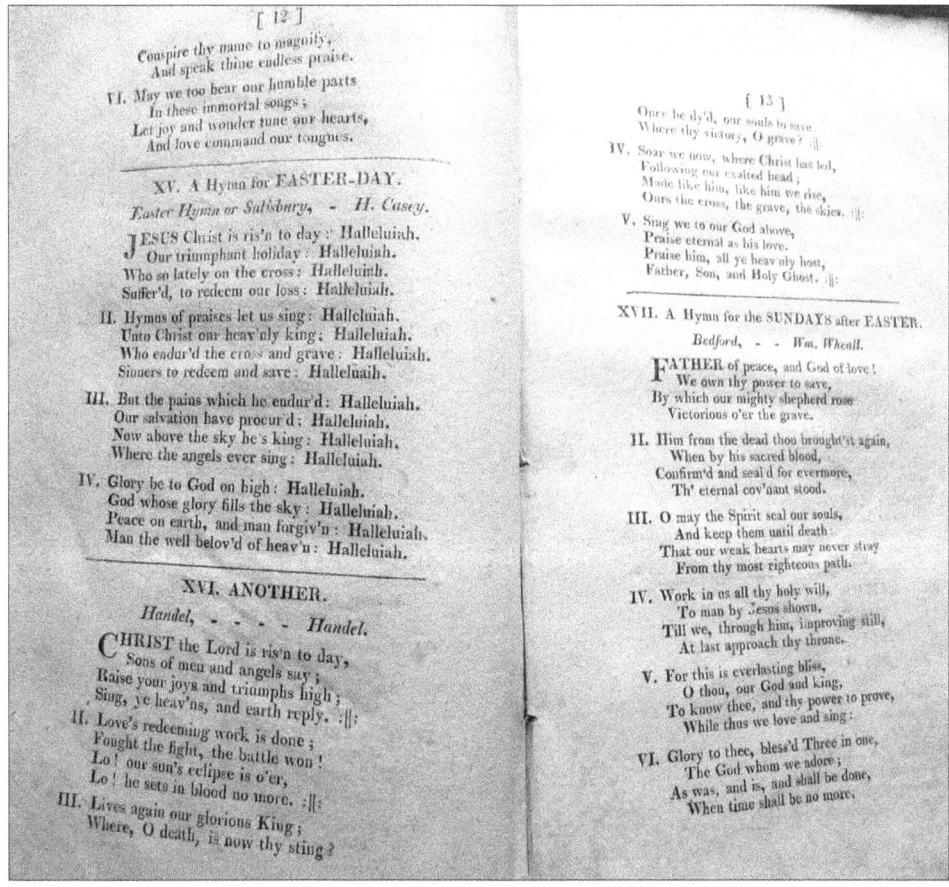

Plate 74. Easter Hymn from an 1824 BCP.

A further occasional but quite frequent addition to the State Services was a service commemorating the accession of the reigning monarch. So, for instance, in a Prayer Book of 1716, there is a service for 5th August in recognition of the accession of George I; in 1735, for 11th June for George II; and in 1763 on 25th October for George III.

A striking feature of some of the eighteenth-century Prayer Books is the inclusion of two sets of Metrical Psalms, the 'old' by Sternhold and Hopkins and the 'new' version by Nahum Tate and Nicholas Brady, in addition to the Coverdale version from the Great Bible. Officially, the Psalter had not been part of the Prayer Book until the 1662 Act of Uniformity. The Psalms of Coverdale have survived revision for three hundred and fifty years, possibly either because they were better adapted to be sung or chanted than later versions or because they could be committed to memory more easily by those who could not read.

Tate and Brady's 'new version' of metrical Psalms appeared in 1696 with a supplement four years later containing music for the Canticles, Creed, Lord's Prayer and six hymns including 'While Shepherds Watched their Flocks by Night'.

The Dissenters, meanwhile, had progressed beyond metrical Psalms, and, under the leadership of Isaac Watts and Charles Wesley, perfected the vernacular congregational hymn.[iii]

IN CONCLUSION

The benefits of the Non-Jurors' liturgical work was appreciated most in Scotland where all the bishops were Non-Jurors from the political point of view. Not all the bishops were of the same mind. Others looked more to the Book of 1637, which was reprinted in its entirety by the Earl of Winton in 1712. The story of the Scottish liturgy will be the subject of the next chapter.

---

iii Cuming, 1969, p. 171.

Chapter 7

SCOTLAND, AMERICA AND IRELAND

THE SCOTTISH COMMUNION OFFICE

Charles I attempted to force the use of the 1637 Prayer Book on the Scottish Church by a highhanded and tactless proclamation. It backfired spectacularly, resulting in the Great Rebellion epitomised by riotous scenes in St Giles, Edinburgh. The upshot was the signing of the National Covenant by a General Assembly carefully packed for the occasion that met in Glasgow Cathedral in 1638.[i]

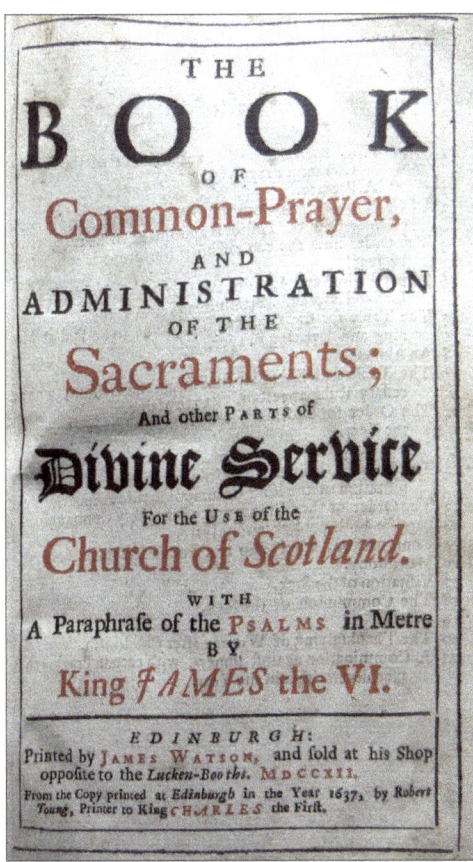

Plate 75. Scottish BCP of 1637 reprinted in 1712. Title page.

One effect of the Glorious Revolution of 1689 was that the Dutch Calvinist William IV formally decreed that the Scots Kirk be Presbyterian in governance. This was established by two statutes 'ratifying the Confession of Faith and Settling Presbyterian Church Government'. This was ratified in the English Act 'for an Union of the Two Kingdoms of England and Scotland' passed in 1707.[ii] The Episcopalians, all Non-Jurors, were obliged to create their own liturgy, which they proceeded to do in a series of pamphlets that became known as 'the wee bookies'. Although the 1637 Prayer Book was never used, it was reprinted, as already noted, by the Earl of Winton in 1712 'for the use of such of the Scottish clergy as might wish to use it'.[iii] Its importance lies in the fact that it is the primary source from which the Scottish Communion Office as used in the Scottish Episcopal Church of today is derived.[iv]

---

i   Campbell, 1949, pp. 17–21.

ii Benton, 1910, p. xxxv.

iii Campbell, 1949, p. 21.

iv Campbell, 1949, p. 22.

The first of the 'wee bookies' appeared in 1722 and consisted of a reprint of the Communion Office of 1637, beginning with the Offertory and omitting the two Exhortations and the rubrics and Collects after the Blessing. Under the leadership of Bishop James Gadderar, many who used the 1637 Communion Office began to alter the order of the prayers. The Prayer for Christ's Church was taken from its place immediately after the Offertory and inserted after the conclusion of the Prayer of Consecration, while the Invitation, Confession, Absolution and Comfortable Words were said at a later stage of the service immediately before the Prayer of Humble Access. These alterations were incorporated in an edition of the 'wee bookies' printed in 1735, in which it claimed that 'all the parts of the Office are ranked in the natural order' – the 'natural order' being that of 1549.[v]

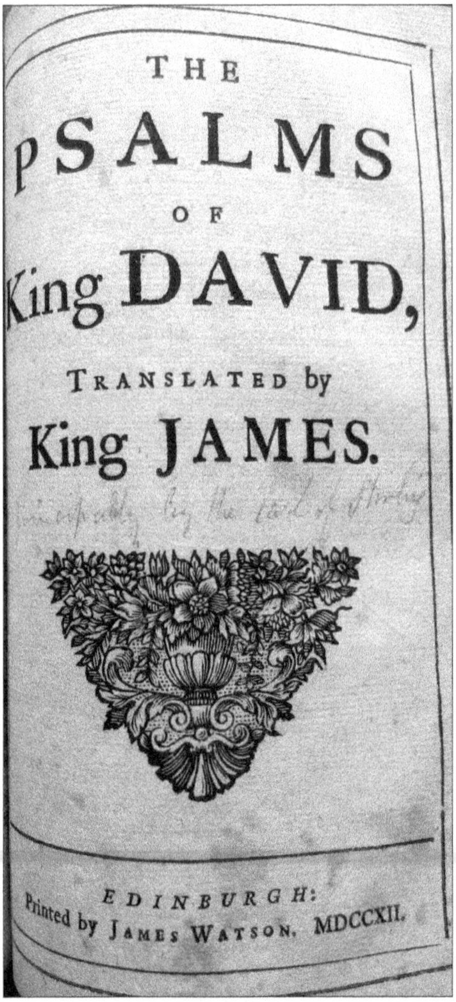

Bishop Thomas Rattray, Primus in 1739, was much influenced by the *Liturgy of St James* from the Eastern Orthodox Church. His work was published posthumously in 1744: 'The Ancient Liturgy of the Church of Jerusalem'. This influenced the wording of later editions of the Scottish Communion Office. The sequence of parts of the Prayer of Consecration, for example, corresponded to the sequence in the Non-Juror's Office of 1718. As in the ancient Liturgies of the East, the recitation of the history of the Institution immediately precedes the Great Oblation, which in its turn precedes the Invocation of the Holy Spirit upon the Elements.

Plate 76. Scottish BCP of 1712. Metrical Psalms attributed to King James but probably translated by the Earl of Stirling.

Rattray's lead was followed in an edition of the Scottish Communion Office issued in 1755 by Bishop William Faulkonar. Faulkonar and Bishop Robert Forbes together issued a further version in 1764, which became the official service of the Episcopal Church of Scotland. It replaced the previous 'wee bookies' and has remained unchanged apart from minor alterations in 1912 and 1929.[vi]

---

v Campbell, 1949, p. 38; Cuming, 1969, p. 187.

vi Cuming, 1969, p. 188; Campbell, 1949, pp. 37–38; Spinks, 2017, p. 118.

THE BOOK OF COMMON PRAYER IN THE UNITED STATES OF AMERICA

The work of the Scottish Episcopalians was to bear fruit in America where the War of Independence had freed the American Church from the Act of Uniformity. Under English Church law, the Bishop of London was responsible for consecrating bishops for the colonies. When Doctor Samuel Seabury, a priest in Connecticut, was elected bishop, he was sent to London to be consecrated. Without an Act of Parliament, he could not receive consecration without taking an oath of allegiance to the English Crown, which he could not do. He travelled north to Scotland where the Nonjuring bishops were under no such constraint. He was consecrated bishop by the Primus and two other bishops in Aberdeen on 15th November 1784. He returned with a copy of the 1764 Scottish Communion Office that had been used at his consecration and a firm request by the Scottish bishops that this be adopted in any subsequent American Prayer Book. In June 1786, a bill was passed by Parliament making it possible for English bishops to consecrate bishops for America, and William White and Samuel Prevoost were consecrated bishop in the chapel of Lambeth Palace. Hence, by 1789, there was a separate House of Bishops in the General Convention that year.

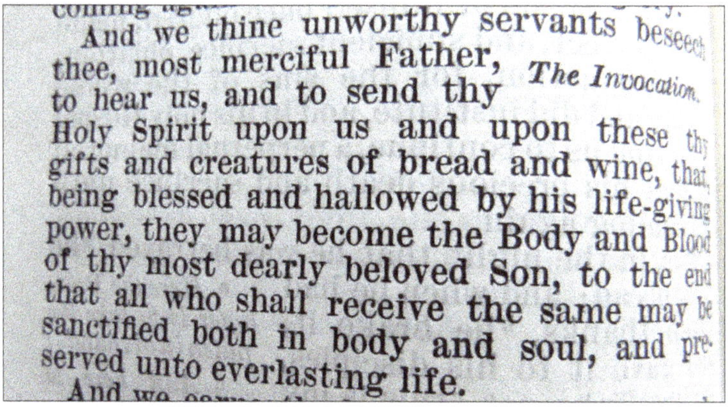
And we thine unworthy servants beseech thee, most merciful Father, to hear us, and to send thy Holy Spirit upon us and upon these thy gifts and creatures of bread and wine, that, being blessed and hallowed by his life-giving power, they may become the Body and Blood of thy most dearly beloved Son, to the end that all who shall receive the same may be sanctified both in body and soul, and preserved unto everlasting life. *The Invocation.*

Plate 77. The Invocation from The Scottish Liturgy in The Scottish Book of Common Prayer 1929. Compare this with the American wording in plate 79.

The Protestant Episcopal Church held a Convention in Philadelphia from 17th September to 7th October 1785, at which were present sixteen clergymen and twenty-six lay deputies representing the States of New York, New Jersey, Pennsylvania, Delaware, Maryland, Virginia and South Carolina. A new Prayer Book was agreed, which became known as 'The Proposed Book'. It was very poorly received and only a few copies were printed, four thousand in Philadelphia by Hall and Sellers in 1786 and fifty in London by J. Debrett in 1789, of which one surviving and rare copy is in Paine's collection. Its main defect was that it omitted the Nicene and Athanasian Creeds, as well as the words 'descended into hell' from the Apostles' Creed and treated the Psalms very freely. In the Marriage rite, everything from the Blessing was deleted; a service for the Visitation of Prisoners from the 1711 version of the Irish Prayer Book was included.

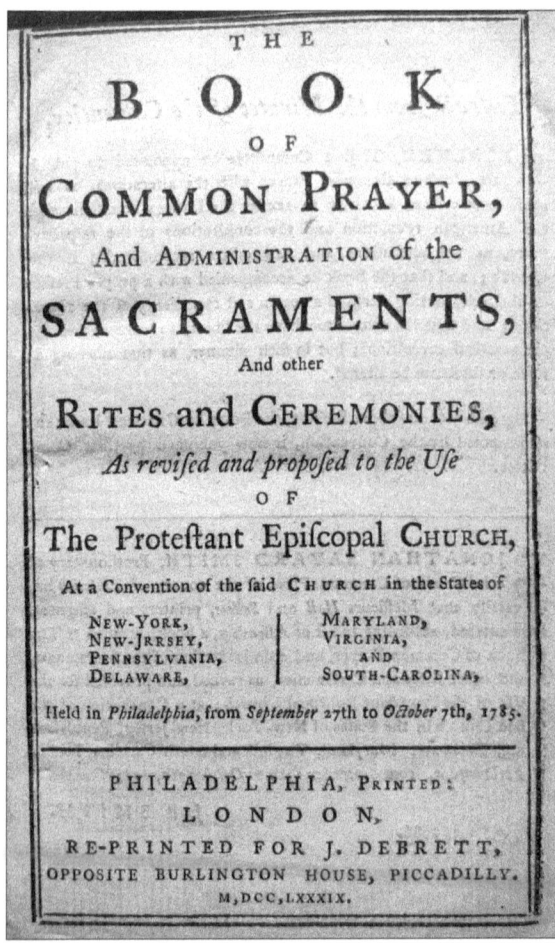

Plate 78. American BCP of 1789 – The Proposed Book. Title page.

The Preface announced: 'It is far from the intention of this Church to depart from the Church of England, any further than local customs require, or to deviate in any thing essential to the true meaning of the 39 Articles.' The word 'priest' was replaced by 'minister' or 'pastor'. Baptismal regeneration was toned down and hymns were introduced by Phillip Doddridge and Samuel Wesley.[vii] Bishop Seabury said that some of the alterations in the book were 'for the worse and most of them not for the better'.

On 28th July 1789, a new Convention of the Episcopal Church met in Philadelphia to prepare a new Prayer Book. Seabury had brought with him a notebook, which contained various new prayers, a form of consecrating churches by Thomas Wilson, Bishop of Sodor and Man, and a Deed of Consecration of a New Church. He also advocated the adoption of the Scottish Communion service prayer of consecration and argued that any liturgical revision should be informed by antiquity. When the Convention reconvened in September, Seabury's proposals were accepted.[viii]

This was a revision of the 1662 *Book of Common Prayer* and was published in 1790. Archaisms are removed, minor abbreviations are permitted, the word 'priest' was restored in some places, and the Commination was discarded. The whole Psalter was restored as was the teaching of baptismal regeneration. New forms are provided for Harvest Thanksgiving, for the Consecration of Churches (published in 1799 and based on Lancelot Andrewes) and for the Institution of Ministers (1804). Further occasional prayers and thanksgivings are added, including one by Jeremy Taylor in the Visitation of the Sick. The Psalms are freely abbreviated and combined, and

---

vii Spinks, 2017, p. 123.

viii Spinks, 2017, p. 124.

hymns are officially recognised. Parents may be accepted as godparents in Baptism.[ix]

Changes in the Communion service reflect the Scottish tradition: 'here in earth' is omitted from the Prayer for the Church Militant, and the rubric on kneeling disappears. The Summary of the Law is borrowed from the Non-Jurors. Most important of all, the Scottish form of the Eucharistic Prayer was adopted at Bishop Seabury's insistence so that oblation and epiclesis precede Communion. The wording of the epiclesis was restored to the form of 1637. In other respects, the English order was followed.[x]

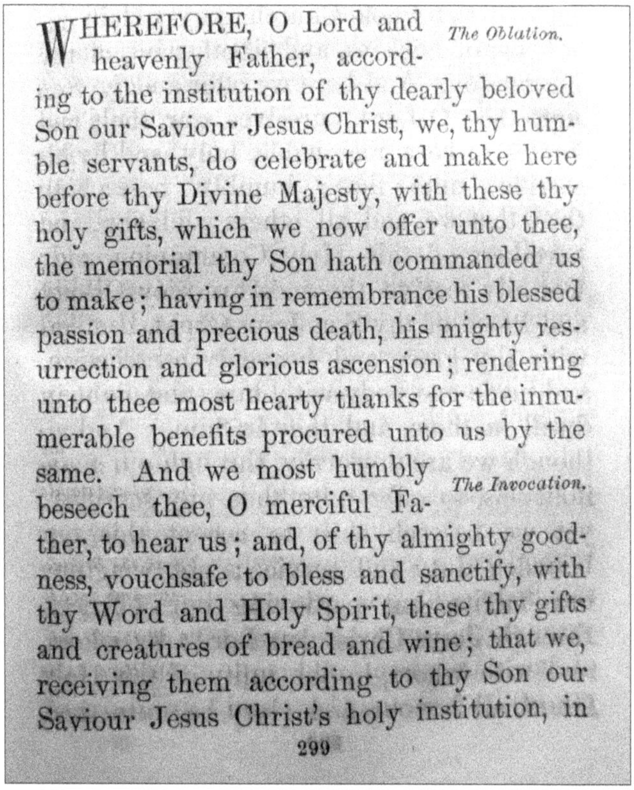

> WHEREFORE, O Lord and heavenly Father, according to the institution of thy dearly beloved Son our Saviour Jesus Christ, we, thy humble servants, do celebrate and make here before thy Divine Majesty, with these thy holy gifts, which we now offer unto thee, the memorial thy Son hath commanded us to make; having in remembrance his blessed passion and precious death, his mighty resurrection and glorious ascension; rendering unto thee most hearty thanks for the innumerable benefits procured unto us by the same. And we most humbly beseech thee, O merciful Father, to hear us; and, of thy almighty goodness, vouchsafe to bless and sanctify, with thy Word and Holy Spirit, these thy gifts and creatures of bread and wine; that we, receiving them according to thy Son our Saviour Jesus Christ's holy institution, in

The Oblation.

The Invocation.

Plate 79. The Oblation and Invocation from an American BCP of 1855.

Marion Hatchett wrote:

> It has been fashionable to minimise the influence of the Proposed Book (1786) upon the Prayer Book of 1789...But the basis of the Preface, Lectionary, Occasional Prayers and Thanksgivings and hymns and the revision of almost every one of the Offices was the version of the Proposed Book.[xi]

The Book was published by Hall and Sellers in 1790. Though the editions of 1790, 1791 and 1792 were not Standard Editions, they were followed by six Standard Editions beginning with that of 1793. The Standard Editions of 1793–1871 were followed by the first Standard Book of 1892 and the second Standard Book of 1928, the three most important being those of 1789, 1892 and 1928.

The Proposed Book of 1786 contained a 'Form of Prayer and Thanksgiving to Almighty God for the Inestimable Blessings of Religion and Civil Liberty' to be used yearly on the fourth day of July. The compilers of 1789 unfortunately failed to incorporate this

---

ix Cuming, 1969, p. 190.

x Cuming, 1969, p. 189.

xi Cited in Spinks, 2017 p. 125.

in the first American Book, but a token of it appears in the Collect and Lessons for Independence Day added in 1928.[xii]

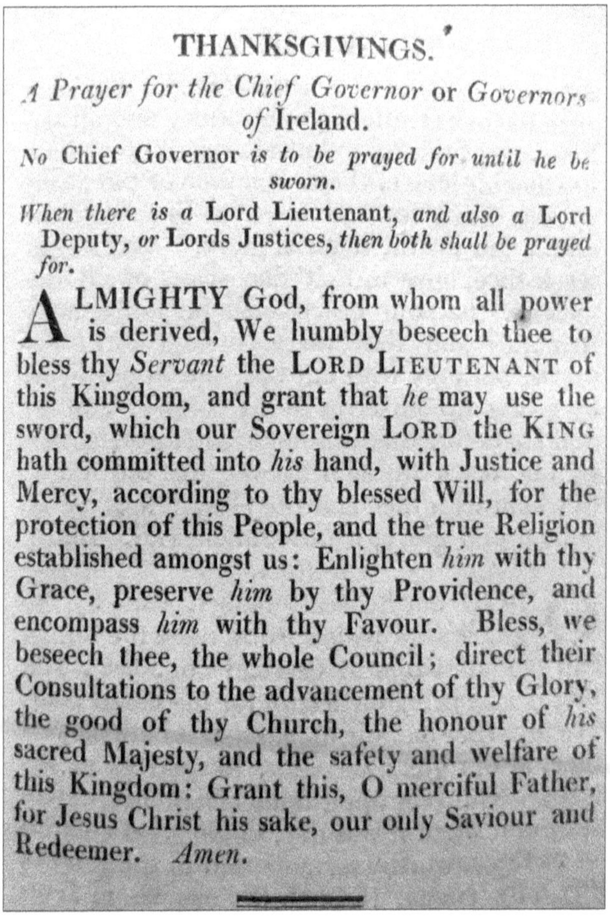
THANKSGIVINGS.

A Prayer for the Chief Governor or Governors of Ireland.

No Chief Governor *is to be prayed for until he be sworn.*

When there is a Lord Lieutenant, *and also a* Lord Deputy, *or* Lords Justices, *then both shall be prayed for.*

ALMIGHTY God, from whom all power is derived, We humbly beseech thee to bless thy *Servant* the LORD LIEUTENANT of this Kingdom, and grant that *he* may use the sword, which our Sovereign LORD the KING hath committed into *his* hand, with Justice and Mercy, according to thy blessed Will, for the protection of this People, and the true Religion established amongst us: Enlighten *him* with thy Grace, preserve *him* by thy Providence, and encompass *him* with thy Favour. Bless, we beseech thee, the whole Council; direct their Consultations to the advancement of thy Glory, the good of thy Church, the honour of *his* sacred Majesty, and the safety and welfare of this Kingdom: Grant this, O merciful Father, for Jesus Christ his sake, our only Saviour and Redeemer. *Amen.*

Plate 80. Prayer for the Lord Lieutenant of Ireland from a BCP of George III.

An innovation of rich spiritual significance in 1789 was the addition of a section called 'Forms of Prayer to be Used in Families'. The prayers were written by the Rt. Rev. Edmund Gibson, Bishop of London, and have remained in subsequent editions. In the 1892 Standard Book, the *Magnificat* and *Nunc Dimittis* were added to Evening Prayer in their traditional positions. A prayer for the President was included as was an additional petition in the Litany 'that it may please thee to send forth labourers into the harvest'. The number of occasional prayers was increased by the present prayer for Unity, which was derived from the 1662 Accession Service, the Prayer for Missions, which was written by Bishop B. P. Cotton of Calcutta in 1861 and revised in 1928, and the Prayer for Fruitful Seasons. A Collect, Epistle and Gospel were provided for the Feast of the Transfiguration which was set for 6th August.[xiii]

THE BOOK OF COMMON PRAYER IN IRELAND

The *Book of Common Prayer* was first printed and used in Ireland in 1551. In 1560, the Irish Parliament passed an Act of Uniformity establishing the *Book of Common Prayer* as it was then established in England. A Latin translation was made by authority of the queen in 1560 but not printed in the Irish language until 1608.

xii Suter and Cleveland, 1949, p. 62.

xiii Suter and Cleveland, 1949, pp. 62–64.

In 1666, the Irish Parliament passed an Act of Uniformity establishing the English *Book of Common Prayer* of 1662 as the service of the Church of Ireland with an addition of a prayer for the Lord Lieutenant of Ireland. A further addition was John Cosin's 'A Form of Consecration of a Church'. In 1700, a further addition was made entitled 'A Form for Receiving Lapsed Protestants, and Reconciling Converted Papists'. A 'Form of Prayer for the Visitation of Prisoners' was agreed upon in 1711 and remained in the book until 1926.

The Act of Union of 1st August 1800 took effect on 1st January 1801 and the title of the Prayer Book adapted to read '...according to the use of the United Church of England and Ireland'. This continued until the disestablishment of the Church in Ireland by Act of Parliament in 1869.[xiv]

---

xiv Benton, 1910 pp. xxxiii–xxxiv; Spinks, 2017, p. 95; Cuming, 1969, p. 170.

APPENDIX 4

THE PRAYERS OF CONSECRATION AND OBLATION IN THE SCOTTISH AND AMERICAN LITURGIES

BCPs 1637 and 1712

Invocation (epiclesis)

Words of Institution

Prayer of Oblation

Anamnesis

Invocation: '…to bless and sanctify with thy Word and Holy Spirit these thy gifts and creatures of bread and wine.'

Anamnesis: '…we thy humble servants do celebrate and make here before thy divine majesty, with these thy gifts, the memorial which thy Son hath willed us to make, having in remembrance…'

Scottish and American Liturgy

Words of Institution

Oblation and anamnesis

Invocation

Following the order of the Non-Juror's Book of 1718.

While the American *Book of Common Prayer*, at least until 1855, maintained the same words as the Scottish liturgies of 1637 and 1712 but the order of the Non-Juror's Book, by 1929 the Scots had new wording. No one used the wording of the Non-Juror's Communion Office 'taken partly from Primitive Liturgies'.

Chapter 8

PRINTERS, PUBLICATIONS AND ILLUSTRATIONS

PRIVATE PRINTERS AND THE ROYAL LICENCE

Prayer books could be bought bound or unbound. The unbound text could then be bound with the owner's name as in the case of the Book of Hours or with the Royal coat of arms. A further reason was that it could be bound with the Bible or New Testament, metrical psalms and/or hymnal.

Plate 81. BCP 1615. Printed by Robert Barker.
Title page to the Psalter.

The first Prayer Books were printed in **blackletter type** in a style known as gothic.[i] There was a gradual change to the familiar roman type, which was first used in 1586. The last blackletter book was issued in 1707. The first Books of Common Prayer were printed by **Richard Grafton** and **Edward Whitchurch**[ii] under the king's licence. They had already published two Bibles: Matthew's of 1537 and Coverdale's in 1538 as well as Henry VIII's Great Bible of 1548. Together, they published four editions of the 1549 book and eleven of the 1552 book. Grafton's Warrant as King's Printer was revoked after he had published a proclamation in favour of Lady Jane Grey, and it was never restored.[iii]

Richard Jugge and John Cawood became the Queen's Printers

---

i   See plates in chapters 1 and 2.
ii See chapter 2, plates 16 and 31.
iii Griffiths, 2002, p. 7.

under Elizabeth. They held the licence until Jugge's death in 1577, when it was acquired by **Christopher Barker**, in whose family it remained for 132 years, passing eventually to John Baskett.

Robert Barker had to sell his shares in the family monopoly to **Bonham Norton** and **John Bill**, who printed Prayer Books from 1623 to 1680 (see plates 61 and 62). The patent was purchased by John Baskett of Oxford in 1709, and in 1717, he became printer to the University of Oxford.

In 1770, the third generation of the Baskett family sold the office of the King's Printer for £10,000 to Mr Charles Eyre of Clapham. Eyre was not a practical printer and therefore sold a third share of the patent to William Strahan. William's third son, Andrew, succeeded his father in 1785, and in the king's letter patent of July 1799 the King's Printers are named as John Reeves, George Eyre and Andrew Strahan. **John Reeves'** name appears on Prayer Book imprints between 1801 and 1815. He had an idiosyncratic approach to printing and was more a publisher than a printer. Between 1801 and 1815, he issued some twenty-five editions of the Prayer Book, each printed by others on his behalf. He often provided a lengthy commentary and altered the order of the contents. As Paine comments after a fulsome dedication to Queen Charlotte (George III's wife) and a sixty-plus-page introduction: 'This Book of Common Prayer is the prime edition given to the Queen and contains Reeves at his most prolific. As time passed the public preferred less of Reeves and more of the B.C.P.'

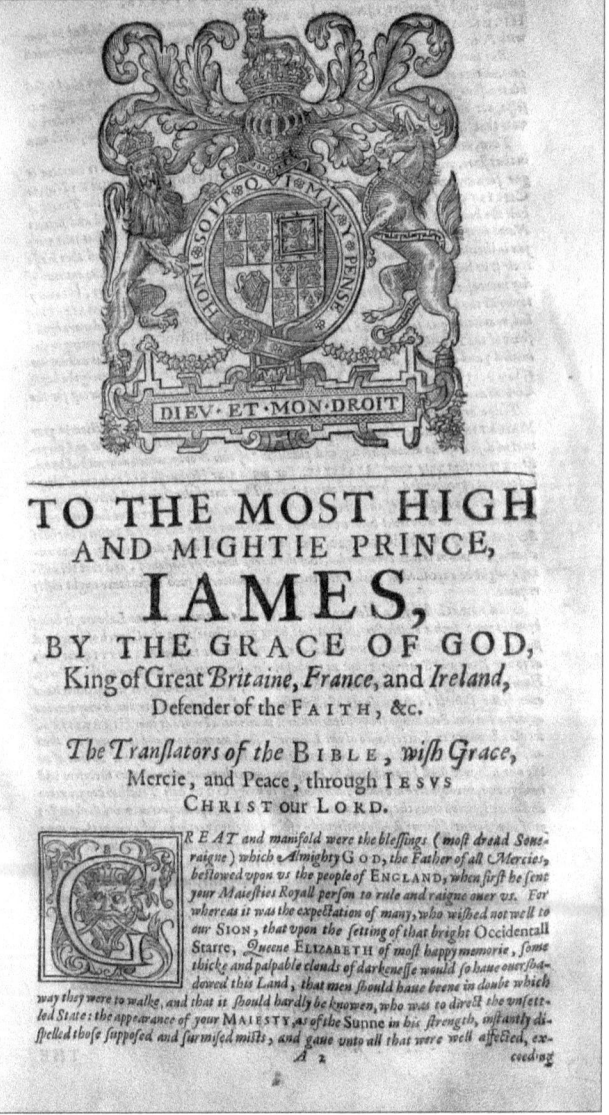

Plate 82. BCP 1629. Norton and Bill. t.p. of the Bible.

Plate 83. 1637 Scottish Prayer Book. 'Cathedral' binding. Folio edition.

When Strahan retired in 1819, he was succeeded by his nephew Andrew and Robert Spottiswoode. Reeves died in 1829 and Robert Spottiswoode in 1832, after which the firm became Eyre and Spottiswoode and continued to hold the Royal Warrant as Queen's Printers until 1990. In that year, the firm's Bible and Prayer Book interests were acquired by the Cambridge University Press.[iv]

THE PRIVILEGED UNIVERSITY PRESSES

The history of printing in both university presses dates back to 1584 when the printers to the queen (or king) had an effective monopoly over the Bible and *Book of Common Prayer*, which continued to the reign of Charles I. A Privy Council decision of April 1629 gave the university printers specific authority to print any number of English Bibles in quarto and medium folio with the liturgy in the same volume and the 'singing psalms' at the end but not to print Prayer Books alone without Bibles. Thus, the first Cambridge edition of the Prayer Book was a folio, bound with the 'authorised' or 'King James' version of the Bible printed by Thomas and Jon Buck, printers to the university in 1629.[v]

John Field,[vi] who printed the 1662 *Book of Common Prayer* in the collection, became printer to the university in 1655. A year after Field's death in 1668, **John Hayes** succeeded him and continued until his death in 1705. **Joseph Bentham** was appointed university printer in 1741.

Plate 84. BCP 1683 M. Pitt for Oxford University. Includes 54 engravings and 33 homilies (see following page for illustrations).

---

iv Griffiths, 2002, p. 9.

v Griffiths, 2002, p. 9.

vi See chapter 5, plate 55.

Plate 85. BCP 1683 'Resurrection'.

Plate 86. BCP 1683. St. John the Apostle.

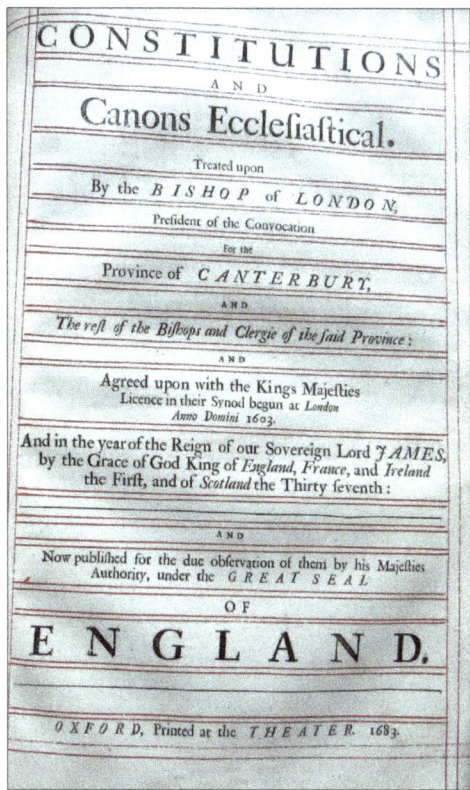

Plate 87. BCP 1683. 'Constitutions and Canons' n.b. James is 37th of Scotland.

Plate 88. BCP 1683 'Certain Sermons and Homilies'. Thirty three of them.

CHAPTER 8: PRINTERS, PUBLICATIONS AND ILLUSTRATIONS

Between 1743 and 1758, there were no less than thirty editions and impressions of the Prayer Book, all printed in Cambridge. In 1758, **John Baskerville** was appointed printer to the University of Cambridge, though he lived and worked in Birmingham. He successfully printed books that were distinctive both in design and workmanship. They became noted for their delicate type, elegant ornaments and hot-pressed impressions on smooth paper. He is still known today by the typeface that bears his name. He presented copies of his Prayer Books to George III and the king's mother,

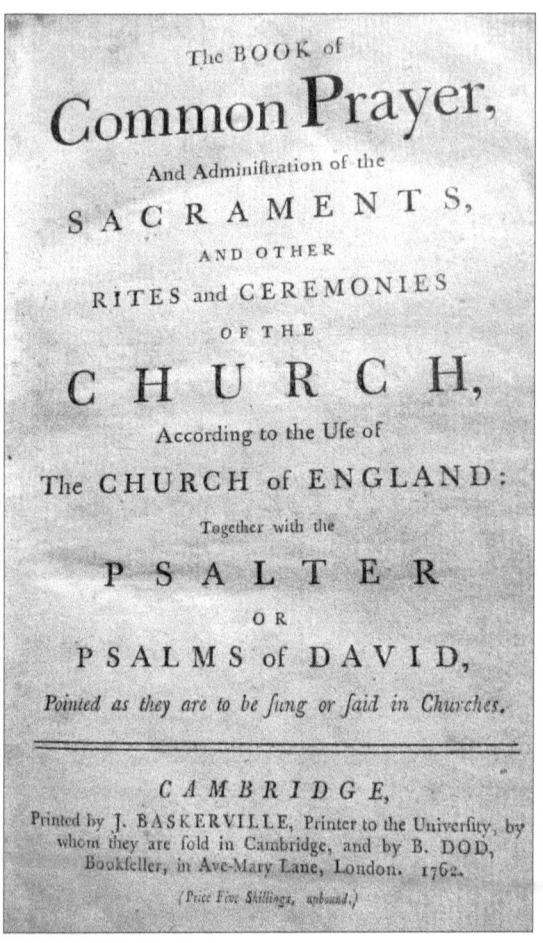

Plate 89. BCP 1762 John Baskerville. t.p.

Plate 90. BCP 1762 John Baskerville. Morning Prayer.

the Princess Dowager of Wales, but he made very little profit.

The university was allowed to appoint up to three printers. In 1766, **John Archdeacon** succeeded Joseph Bentham. He was prepared to experiment with a new typefounder. He died in 1795 and was succeeded by John Burges, who took over at a time of political and technological revolution when the effects of war and the French Revolution coincided with the introduction of machine-made paper, the iron press and the stereotype.[vii]

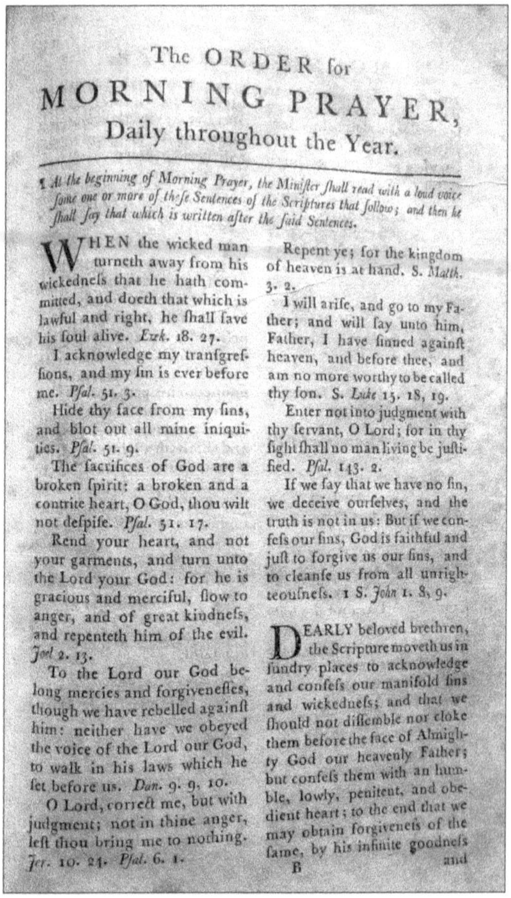

---

vii Griffiths, 2002, p. 11.

Plate 91. BCP 1716 John Baskett. English 18th c. fine morocco binding tooled in gilt with silver clasps.

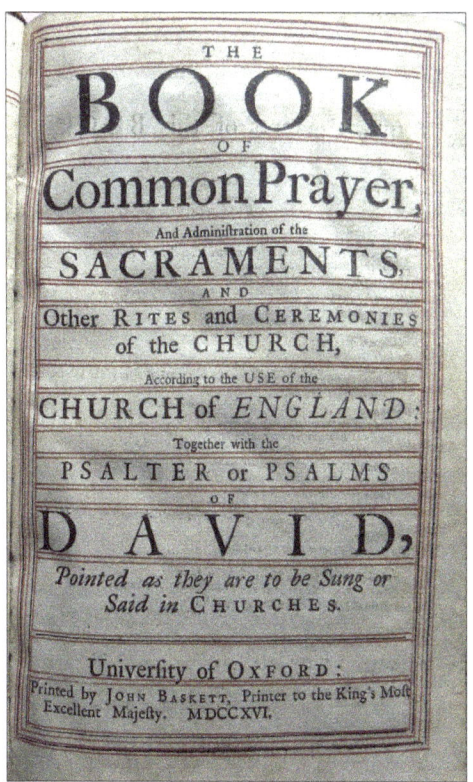

Plate 92. BCP 1716 John Baskett. t.p.

Plate 93. BCP 1716 J. Baskett. Hand painted illustration of 'Cranmer' opposite t.p.

Plate 94. BCP 1716 J. Baskett. St. James the Great dressed as a pilgrim to Santiago de Compostela.

CHAPTER 8: PRINTERS, PUBLICATIONS AND ILLUSTRATIONS

Plate 95. BCP 1716 J. Baskett.
St. Luke the Evangelist.

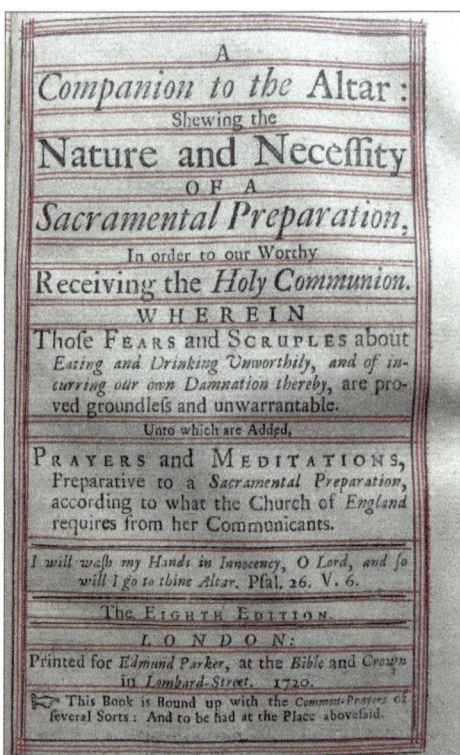

Plate 96. BCP 1716. J. Baskett. A Companion to the Altar. Printed by Edmund Parker in 1720 and inserted between Holy Communion and Baptism.

Plate 97. BCP 1716 J. Baskett. The Last Supper. Opposite A Companion to the Altar.

Plate 98. BCP 1716 J. Baskett. 'Cottage' binding tooled in gilt.

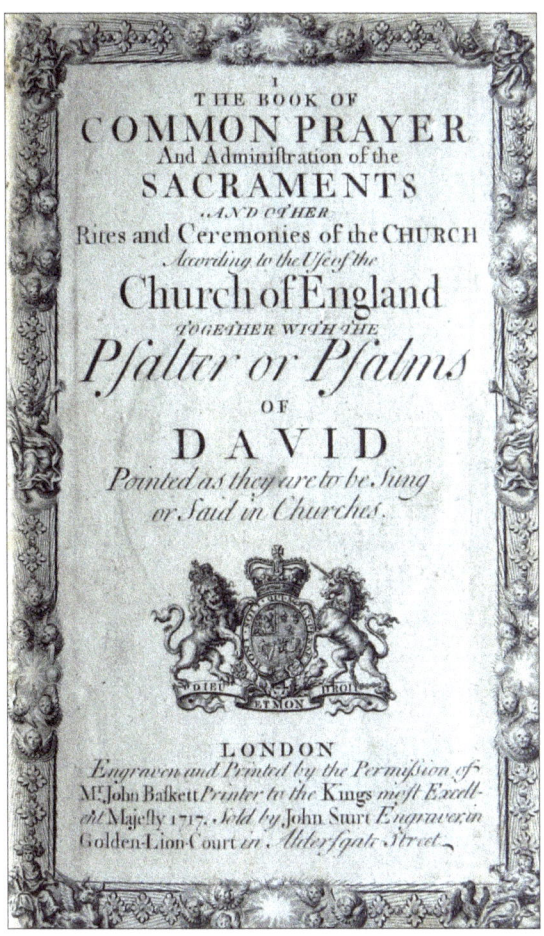

Plate 99. BCP 1717. Baskett and Sturt.

Baskett, who had become printer to the University of Oxford in 1717, was not much interested in the process of printing and spent much of his time in litigation aimed at promoting his own fortunes and prohibiting others from acquiring printing rights. A contemporary pamphlet gives a colourful account of the state of his works at the time:

> Mr. Baskett lived upon a genteel private fortune and neither understood nor gave any attention to the business of printing. He left it therefore to the care of servants...The underservants and press men were a set of idle drunken men, and the house appeared more like an ale house than a printing room.[viii]

Nevertheless, Baskett produced some of the finest books in the collection, including one of 1716 with forty-two engraved, hand-coloured plates, the bilingual edition with royal binding (1717), one of 1725 with 'The Liturgy of the Church of England adorned with 55 New Historical Cuts' and the Non-Juror's book of 1727.

Plate 100. BCP 1717. Baskett and Sturt. The bust of King George I in which is inscribed the Prayers for the King and Royal Family, Psalm 23, The Lord's Prayer, the Creed and Ten Commandments.

viii Griffiths, 2002, p. 13.

Plate 101. BCP 1787. John Archdeacon. Charles I.

Plate 102. BCP 1787. John Archdeacon. Charles II.

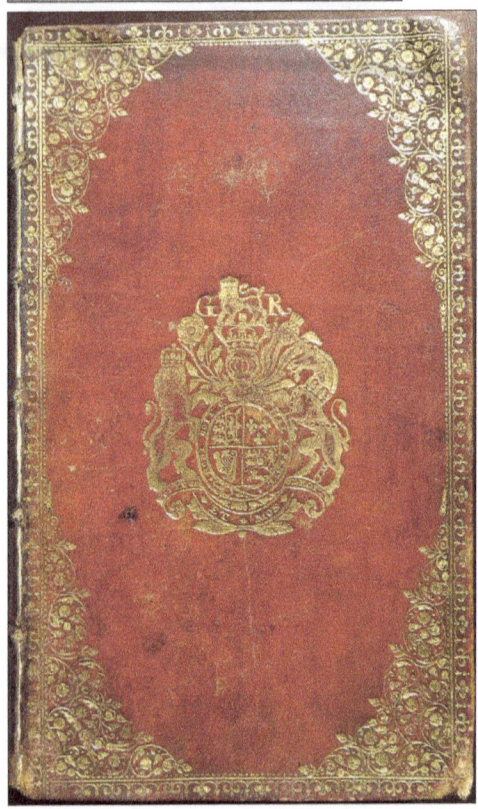

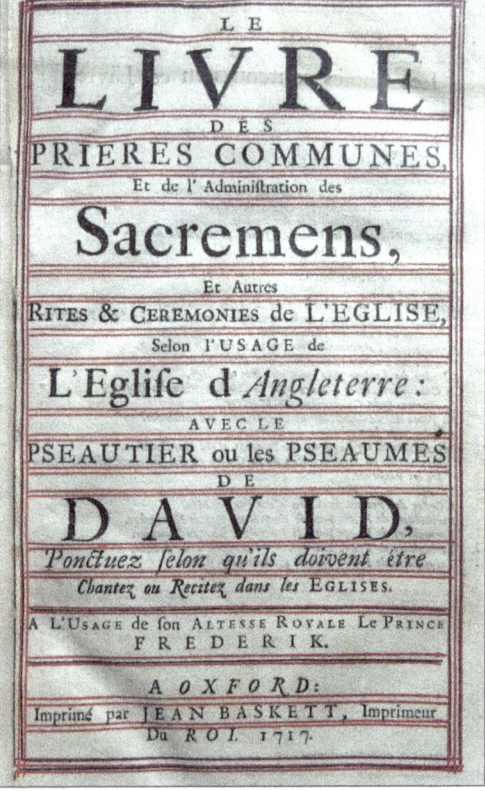

Plate 103. BCP 1717. Le Livre des Prieres Communes. Arms of George I.

Plate 104. BCP 1717 Le Livre des Prieres Communes. t.p.

Plate 105. BCP 1801 John Reeves. Red morocco English binding, tooled in gilt.

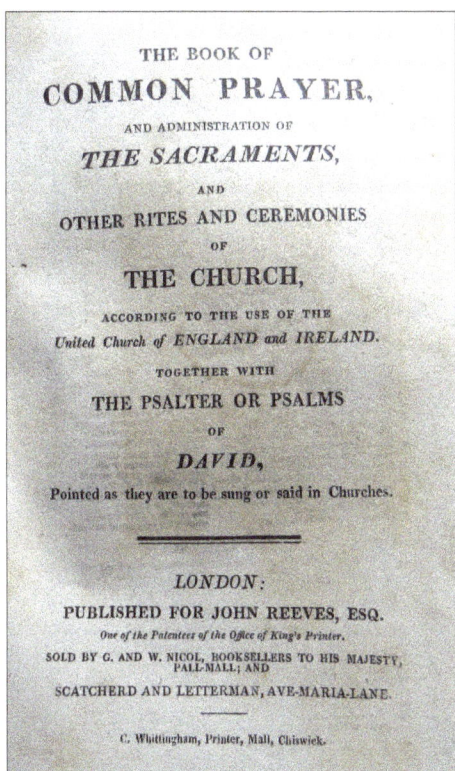

Plate 106. BCP 1801 John Reeves. t.p.

Plate 107. BCP 1801 John Reeves. 'Going to Church'. one of nine similar engravings.

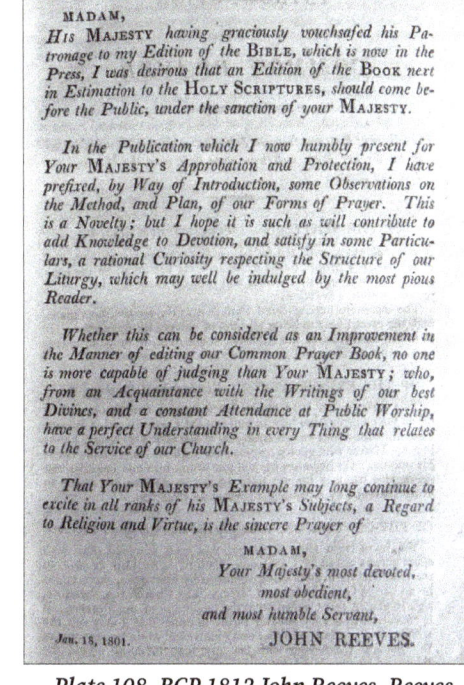

Plate 108. BCP 1812 John Reeves. Reeves dedicated all his publications to Queen Charlotte and dated them 1801.

CHAPTER 8: PRINTERS, PUBLICATIONS AND ILLUSTRATIONS

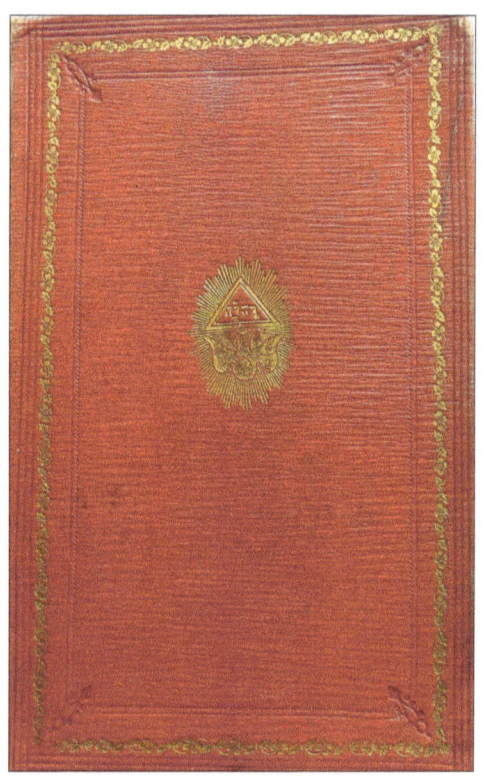

*Plate 109. BCP 1815 John Reeves.
Fine red morocco tooled in gilt.
Symbol of God and a dove in glory.*

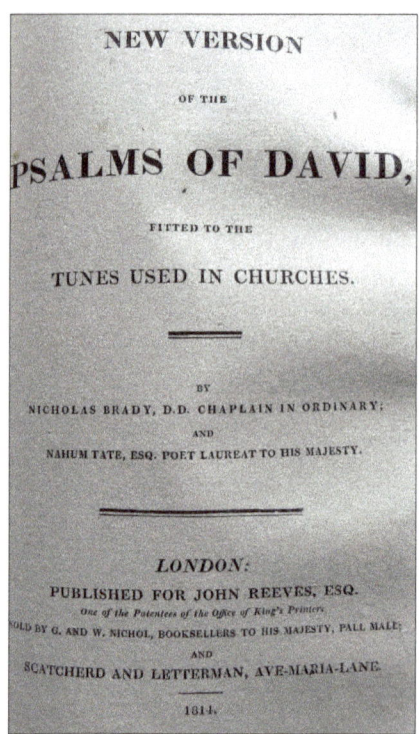

*Plate 110. BCP 1815 Reeves.
A New Version of the Psalms of David by
Nicholas Brady D.D. and Nahum Tate
Esq. Poet Laureat to his Majesty.*

*Plate 111. BCP 1815 Reeves.
Engraving of Raphael's 'Madonna'
published by S. Leigh opp. t.p.*

*Plate 112. BCP 1815 Reeves.
Rubens' 'Nativity' opp. Christmas lections.
One of five unique engravings.*

Mark Baskett, who had succeeded his father in 1742, had the lease withdrawn by the university, and it went to Thomas Wright and William Gill, stationers in the City of London. This lease expired in 1799 when, with rising standards, it was replaced by a partnership between the Syndics of the Press and two printers: Archibald Harrison of Fleet Street and **William Jackson** in Oxford. The partnership between the university and outside firms lapsed in 1836 and was replaced by full-time, salaried officers of the university.[ix]

One successful production by **John Baskett** in conjunction with **John Sturt** was the subscription octavo edition of 1717 (see plates 99 and 100). The typeface (approximately 5.25 point) was engraved on 189 silver plates with engraved borders of varying designs and decorated with vignettes and initials. The two copies in the collection both include an intact volvelle with a circular table to find the dates of the movable Sundays of the year. A list of the subscribers is printed and the Psalter in three columns as well as a list of Sturt's other publications.

MISCELLANEOUS PUBLICATIONS

Much Prayer Book publishing as opposed to printing had been taken over by the **Society for Promoting Christian Knowledge** founded in 1698. By 1745, the SPCK was a sufficiently important customer to examine Mr (Thomas) Baskett's Bibles and Prayer Book misprints, and in 1791, no fewer than fifty-eight different Prayer Book editions were listed in its catalogue. One of those is a commemorative edition celebrating the diamond jubilee of Queen Victoria in 1897. After the title page, it includes 'A Form of Prayer of Thanksgiving to Almighty God to be used...upon Sunday the 20th Day of June 1897.' An edition printed for the SPCK has a special binding with the figure of faith on the front and rear covers surrounded by the name and founding date of the Society.

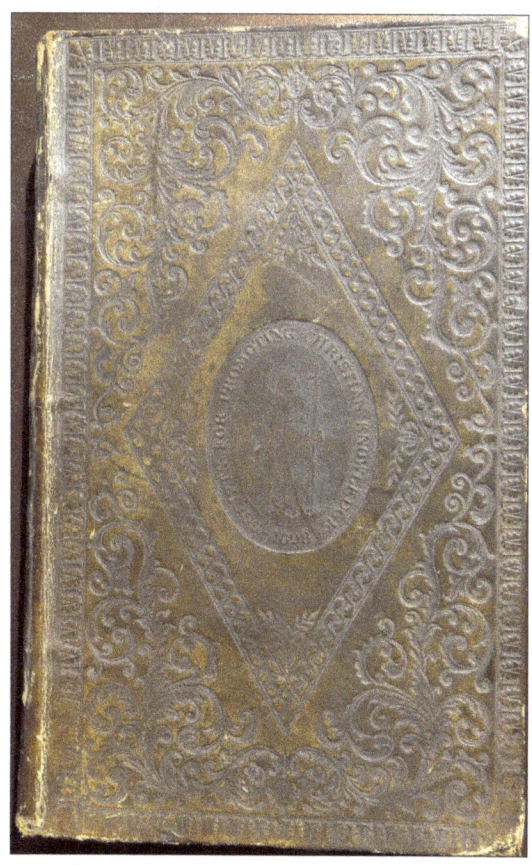

Plate 113. BCP 1840. John W. Parker printer to the University of Cambridge for the Society for Promoting Christian Knowledge. 'The Figure of Faith' 1698.

---

ix Griffiths, 2002, p. 13.

Plate 114. Sarum Psalter printed by Joseph Masters in 1852.

In 1844, William Pickering published an authoritative modern luxury edition of seven historic English Prayer Books ranging from 1549 to 1662, including **Merbecke's** 'Book of Common Prayer Noted (1550)'.[x] In 1852, Joseph Masters of Aldersgate Street in the City of London publish a fine-bound English edition of 'The Psalter, or Seven Ordinary Hours of Prayer according to the use of The Illustrious and Excellent Church of Sarum' for the principal feasts and seasons with musical notation and melodies, together with hymns and other devotions; also the Litany and Vigils of the Dead.

In 1871, Longman of London issued a photo-zincographed facsimile of the 1636 blackletter Prayer Book used in 1661 at the Savoy Conference with alterations made in Sancroft's writing.[xi] Three hundred facsimile copies of the 1549 *Book of Common Prayer* printed on handmade paper were reproduced privately in 1896. The Henry Bradshaw Society, founded in 1890, published a facsimile copy of 'The Order of the Communion 1548' in 1908, edited by H. A. Wilson, Fellow of Magdalen College Oxford, and other 'Rare Liturgical Texts'.

Of Prayer Book translations, an unofficial Latin translation was published in Leipzig in 1551, and an unofficial French version appeared in London in 1553. Some show of legal recognition was given to the French version of the 1662 book intended for the

Plate 115. Sarum Psalter 1852. Fine bound by the Guild of Women Binders. Front pastedown.

---

x See chapter 2, plate 25.

xi See chapter 5, plate 53.

use both of the French-speaking churches in the Channel Islands and also by the 'conforming' Huguenot congregations on the British mainland. In 1770, there were seven Huguenot congregations in London licensed by the Bishop of London and nine in the coastal towns south of a line from the Wash to the Bristol Channel.

In 1636, Archbishop Richard Neile of York enquired whether the King's Printer could be 'commanded to imprint them in both languages' (i.e. English and French). One such edition was printed by John Baskett in Oxford: *Le Livres des Prieres Communes* (see plates 103 and 104). The binding bears the crest of King George I and was the possession of the Rt. Revd Robert Trefusis, suffragan bishop of Crediton. The two languages are printed in adjacent columns throughout.

Plate 116. BCP 1853 William Pickering. t.p.

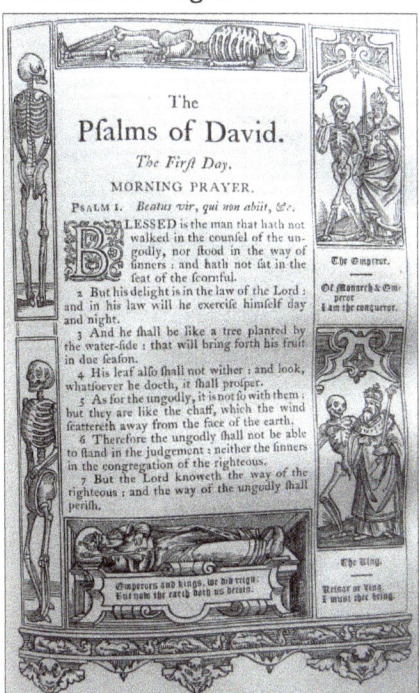

Plate 117. BCP 1853 William Pickering. Psalter with macabre illustrated margins throughout.

The French version authorised for the Savoy Chapel and other French 'conforming' churches included a Royal Warrant countersigned by the Domestic Chaplain to the Bishop of London. This was a reminder that the bishop of London claimed an 'ex officio' jurisdiction over English churches overseas.

A fourth State Service, the Accession Service, was added in 1704, although there had been prayers of thanksgiving in use since the Reformation in every reign. The service was amended by Convocation on 9th November 1901 and authorised by Royal Warrant. It continues to be printed as an annex.

The first stereotyped Cambridge *Book of Common Prayer* was issued on 3rd July 1805; the first Oxford edition in 1806.[xii]

---

xii Griffiths, 2002, p. 219.

Special editions of the Prayer Book were issued for the coronation service of the Sovereign. Examples in the collection include those of 1902, 1911, 1937 and 1953. A Cathedral Prayer Book was published in 1925 with musical settings for all the sung parts of the services including the Psalter.

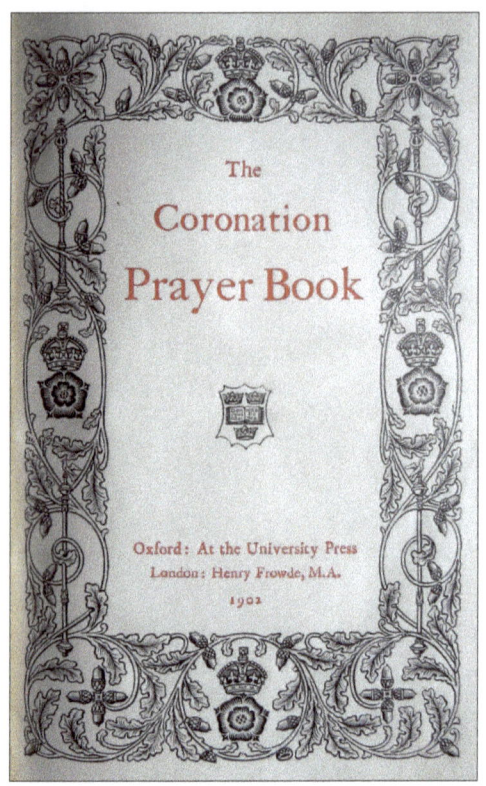

Plate 118. Coronation Prayer Book 1902. t.p.

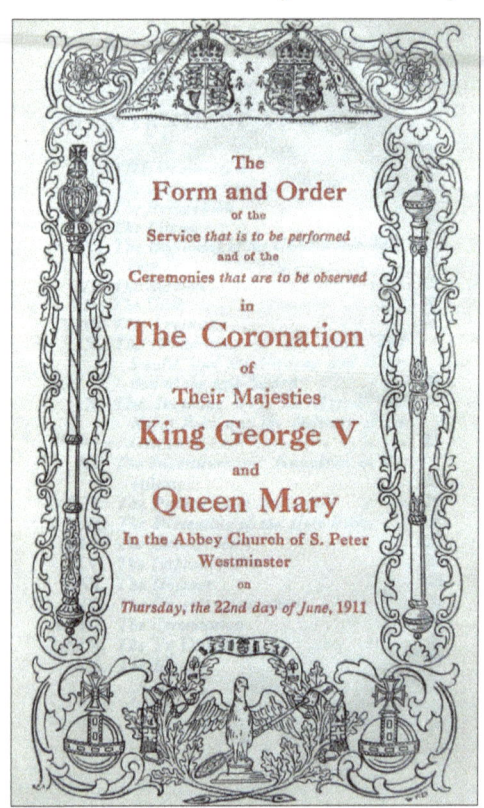

Plate 119. Coronation BCP 1911. Third t.p.

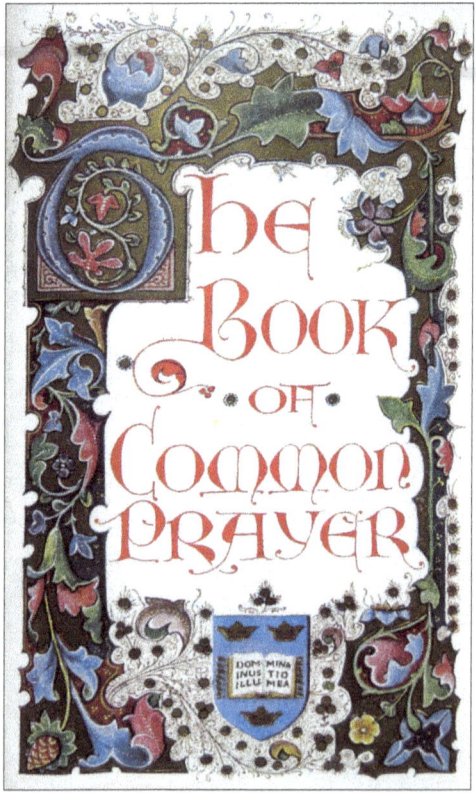

Plate 120. Coronation BCP 1911. Second t.p.

Chapter 9

PRAYER BOOK REVISION IN THE NINETEENTH AND TWENTIETH CENTURIES

Worship according to the *Book of Common Prayer* experienced its high-water mark in the nineteenth century. What brought it to such prominence was the Tractarian Movement, whose proponents encouraged disciplined use of Morning and Evening Prayer not only for the clergy as prescribed by the book but also the laity.

The Tractarians were not uncritical of the Prayer Book and demanded the separation of the three parts of the morning service, matins, litany and ante-communion, into three separate services.

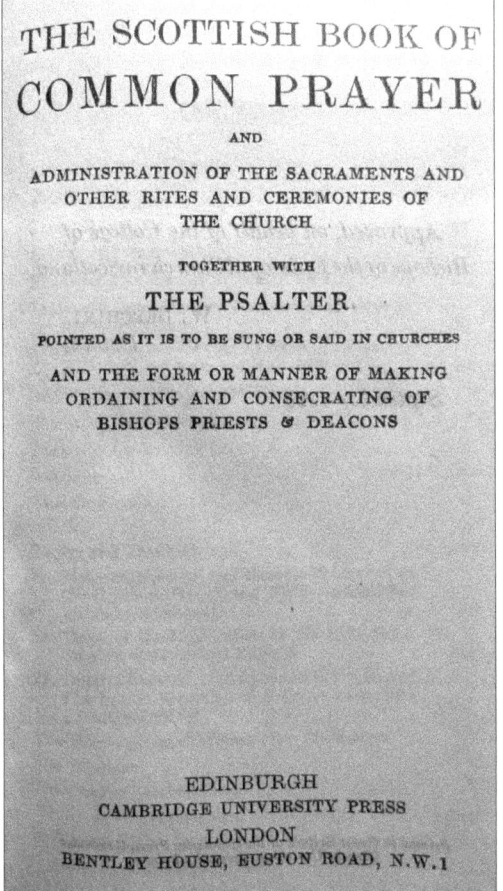

Plate 121. The Scottish Book of Common Prayer 1929 t.p.

In 1839, John Mason Neale and Benjamin Webb founded the Camden Society. Through their periodical *The Ecclesiologist*, they promoted the restoration of churches along medieval lines. A catalyst for this was the Ornaments Rubric of the 1559 Prayer Book. This stated that those ornaments were permitted which were in use in the second year of the reign of Edward VI. There was controversy concerning whether the reference referred to the practice before or after the publication of the 1549 Book and which ornaments were implied. J. M. Neale was much exercised by this question and wrote to a friend in 1844 that the Tract writers had missed one great principle: aesthetics.[i] He claimed that the Ornaments Rubric implied continuity of practice with the Roman Catholic Church, the Eastern Churches and the patristic era.

The consequence of this movement was the reintroduction of stone altars raised nine steps above the nave, the abandonment

---

i Jacobs, 2013, p. 141.

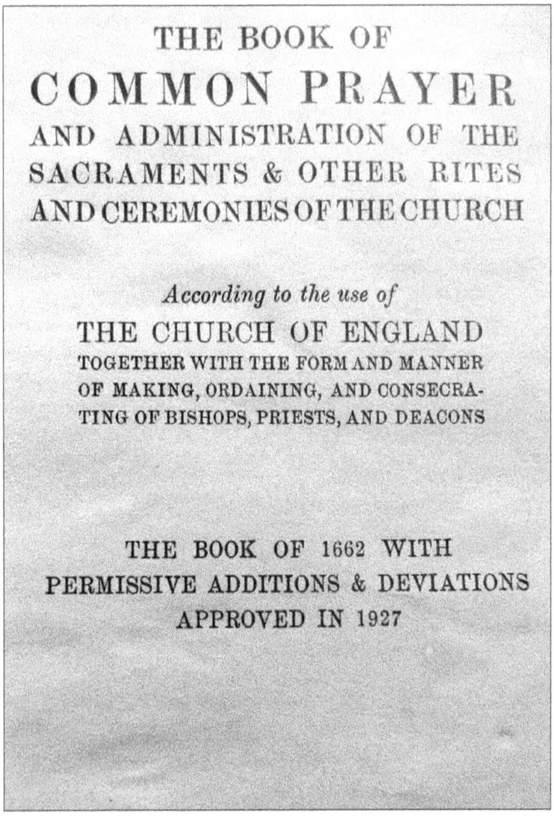

Plate 122. 1927 BCP with Permitted Additions and Deviations t.p.

of box pews and three-decker pulpits and the introduction of pews facing east, and a simple pulpit and lectern. The choir was brought down from the western gallery and placed in the chancel in robes. Organs replaced orchestras, and hymns were gradually replacing the metrical psalms. The first edition of *Hymns Ancient and Modern* appeared in 1860.

In 1857, the Judicial Committee of the Privy Council indicated that in their view, the Ornaments Rubric allowed the use of vestments including the chasuble, altar lights, flowers and incense. However, in 1871, they declared Eucharistic vestments, the eastward position, the mixed chalice, and wafer breads all to be unlawful which was deeply unacceptable to Tractarian sensitivities.

The State Services came in for much criticism not only from the Tractarians but also from F.D. Maurice and Dean Milman of St Paul's. In 1858, Parliament debated the matter, and the queen approved their withdrawal from the Prayer Book by Royal Warrant in January 1859. Around this time, Convocation began to make provision for Harvest Festivals. In 1871, Convocation and then Parliament approved revision of the lectionary. The New Testament was rearranged to be read twice a year instead of three times, and proper lessons were provided for holy days including Ash Wednesday and the whole of Holy Week. The fourth and final report adopted by Convocation recommended 'alterations which may give facilities for adapting the services of the church to the wants and circumstances of different congregations'. Here was the first official divergence from the ideal of 'one use'.[ii]

The first legal variation of the text of the *Book of Common Prayer* came with the passing in 1872 of the Act of Uniformity Amendment Act, which permitted the service of Morning and Evening Prayer to be shortened on weekdays and gave permission for a special service on special occasions provided they were biblically and Prayer Book based. This legitimised the Evangelical practice of extra-liturgical mission services.

---

ii Cuming, 1969, pp. 193–200.

The Public Worship Regulation Act, passed in 1874, failed to resolve the Ornaments Rubric controversy and resulted in the prosecution and conviction of several priests for High Church practices. Most notable among them was Edward King, Bishop of Lincoln, against whom a suit was brought by the Church Association in 1888 to test the legality of six usages. Archbishop Benson found in favour of most of them apart from the use of the sign of the cross at the Absolution and Blessing. These prosecutions were deeply unpopular and were ceased in the early twentieth century, but the Act was not repealed until 1965.[iii]

Disestablishment of the Church in Ireland in 1871 resulted in a reaction against Tractarianism and towards an identity more clearly evangelical than Roman Catholic in its practices. A revision of the Prayer Book in Ireland was published in 1877.

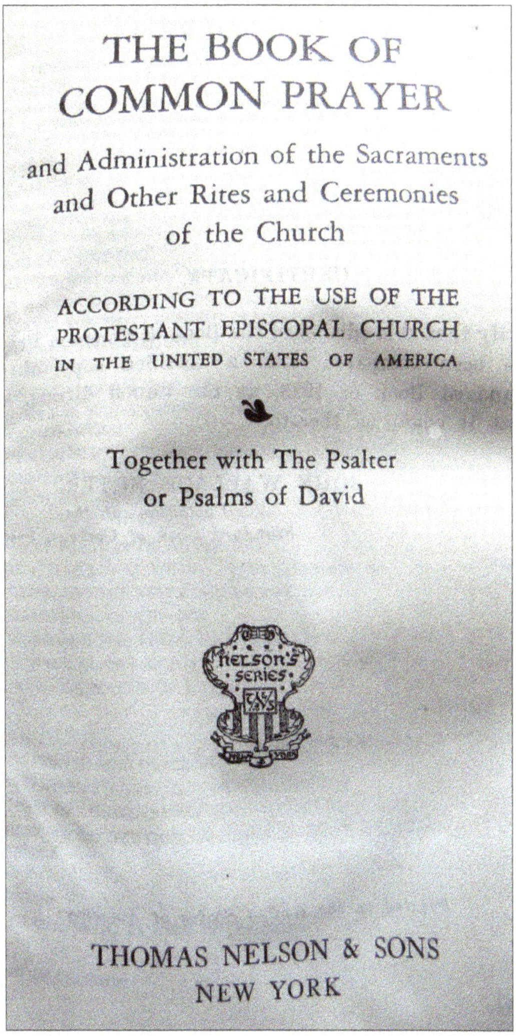

The Protestant Episcopal Church in the United States of America revised its liturgy in 1892. Its links through Bishop Seabury's consecration in Scotland with the Non-Juror's high church traditions and omission of the Ornaments Rubric from their Prayer Book meant that they were unrestrained from continuing their fairly high church practices. The new book was conservative in its changes. The feast of the Transfiguration was

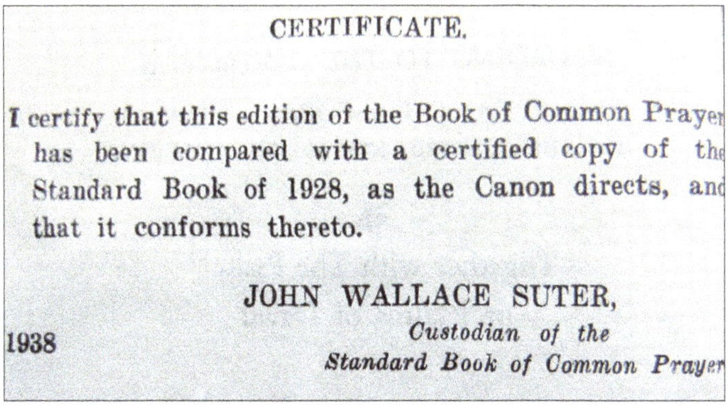

Plate 124. BCP of Protestant Episcopal Church of the USA 1938 t.p.

Plate 123. BCP of Protestant Episcopal Church of the USA 'Certificate'.

---

iii Jacobs, 2013, p. 145.

> NOTE.—*If the Prayer Book Measure, 1928, had received the Royal Assent, the following would have been printed as the title of this Book:*
> THE BOOK OF COMMON PRAYER AND ADMINISTRATION OF THE SACRAMENTS AND OTHER RITES AND CEREMONIES OF THE CHURCH ACCORDING TO THE USE OF THE CHURCH OF ENGLAND TOGETHER WITH THE FORM AND MANNER OF MAKING, ORDAINING, AND CONSECRATING OF BISHOPS, PRIESTS, AND DEACONS   THE BOOK OF 1662 WITH ADDITIONS AND DEVIATIONS APPROVED IN 1928
>
> v

Plate 125. BCP 1928 'Note' of title page had Parliament approved it.

included, the *Nunc Dimittis* and *Magnificat* were restored as were previously omitted parts of the *Benedictus*. New Collects and prayers were added together with the *Kyries* and ten new selections of Psalms. Increased flexibility was permitted especially regarding hymns and metrical psalmody. It was noted that in comparison with 1789, its contents were slightly richer, its style restrained Tudor and its tone distinctly conservative.[iv]

Meanwhile in England during the 1890s, services from other sources than the *Book of Common Prayer* were being used. Many of these were controversial, particularly the veneration of the cross on Good Friday. In 1904, a Royal Commission on Ecclesiastical Discipline was appointed. It concluded that the law in public worship was too narrow for the religious life of the current generation and that discipline had broken down. It recommended greater flexibility of practice and clearer means to enforce it. The way was now open for revision of the Prayer Book after nearly 250 years of its use.

During the following twenty years, schismatic changes took place affecting the Church and State, the greatest of which was the First World War. Army chaplains returned from the

> AN ALTERNATIVE ORDER FOR
> # MORNING PRAYER
> DAILY THROUGHOUT THE YEAR
>
> ¶ *The Minister kneeling shall say or sing:*
> O Lord, open thou our lips;
> *Answer.* And our mouth shall shew forth thy praise.
> *Minister.* O God, make speed to save us;
> *Answer.* O Lord, make haste to help us.
>
> *Here, all standing up, the Minister shall say,*
> Glory be to the Father, and to the Son : and to the Holy Ghost;
> *Answer.* As it was in the beginning, is now, and ever shall be : world without end. Amen.
> *Minister.* Praise ye the Lord;
> *Answer.* The Lord's name be praised.
>
> ¶ *Then shall be said or sung this Psalm following: except on Easter Day and seven days after, when Proper Anthems are appointed to be said in place thereof. And except that on the nineteenth day of every month (not being a day for which one of the Invitatories following is appointed) it is not to be read here, but in the ordinary course of the Psalms.*
>
> ¶ *The* Venite *may be omitted except on Sundays and other Holy-days.*
>
> VENITE, EXULTEMUS DOMINO
> Psalm 95.
>
> O COME, let us sing unto the Lord : let us heartily rejoice in the strength of our salvation.
> 2 Let us come before his presence with thanksgiving : and shew ourselves glad in him with psalms.
> 3 For the Lord is a great God : and a great King above all gods.
> 4 In his hand are all the corners of the earth : and the strength of the hills is his also.
> 5 The sea is his, and he made it : and his hands prepared the dry land.
> 6 O come, let us worship, and fall down : and kneel before the Lord our Maker.
> 7 For he is the Lord our God : and we are the people of his pasture, and the sheep of his hand.
>
> 95

Plate 126. BCP 1928 Morning Prayer, alternative form.

---

iv Spinks, 2017, p. 155.

Front claiming that the language of the Prayer Book no longer communicated with the troops. They also understood the need for the reserved sacrament. A further contributing factor for change besides ongoing pressure from the high and low wings of the church was the contribution of scholarship.

> APPENDIX
>
> An Order for Prime.
> An Order for Compline.
> A Devotion before the celebration of Holy Communion.
> The Collects, Epistles, and Gospels of the Lesser Feasts and Fasts, and other Days.
> An Exhortation.

Plate 127. BCP 1928 Appendix.

In this regard Pearcy Dearmer and Walter H. Frere played a significant role, as did F.E. Brightman, who published *The English Rite* in 1915.

The revised Book presented by the House of Bishops was passed by the Church Assembly. The clergy and laity approving it by 59%; 517 votes to 183 with the Anglo-Catholics and Evangelicals opposing it for opposite reasons. It was presented to Parliament in December 1927 where it was passed in the House of Lords but defeated in the Commons by 238 votes to 205. A majority of English members were in favour, but it was defeated by those from constituencies to whom the measure did not apply. The following year, the bishops presented a revised form to the Synod where it was again accepted but again rejected by the Commons with a slightly higher majority.

Plate 128. Book of Common Order. Church of Scotland 1952 t.p.

The result of this impasse was the issue by the bishops of a statement declaring the Church's 'inalienable right...to arrange the expression' of its faith 'in its forms of worship'. The new Book was published at the end of the year with a note to the effect that publication did not imply authorisation for use in churches, and permission to use any part of the 1928 book would require assent by the Parochial Church Council.

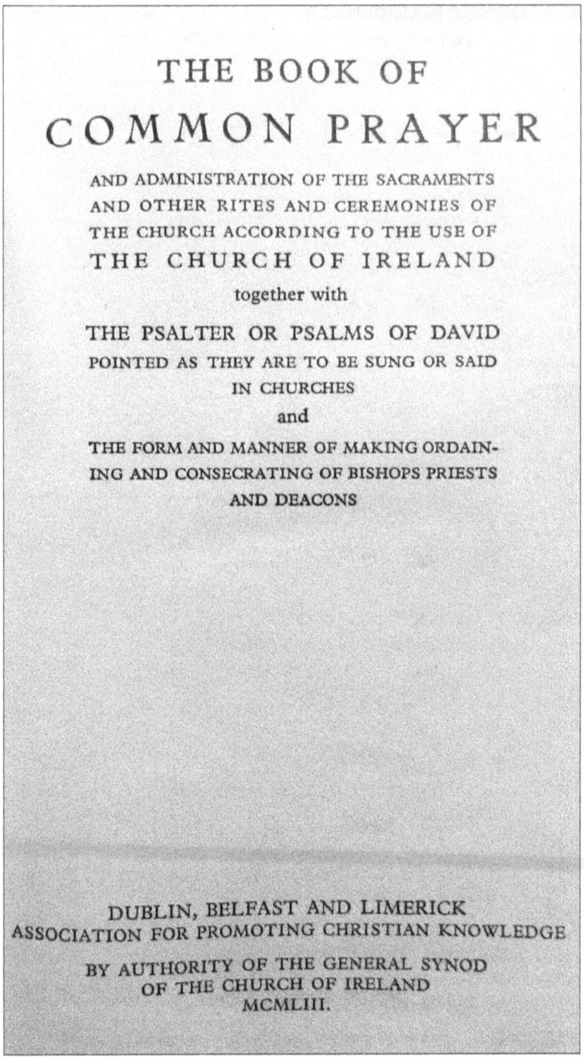
THE BOOK OF
COMMON PRAYER
AND ADMINISTRATION OF THE SACRAMENTS
AND OTHER RITES AND CEREMONIES OF
THE CHURCH ACCORDING TO THE USE OF
THE CHURCH OF IRELAND
together with
THE PSALTER OR PSALMS OF DAVID
POINTED AS THEY ARE TO BE SUNG OR SAID
IN CHURCHES
and
THE FORM AND MANNER OF MAKING ORDAINING AND CONSECRATING OF BISHOPS PRIESTS
AND DEACONS

DUBLIN, BELFAST AND LIMERICK
ASSOCIATION FOR PROMOTING CHRISTIAN KNOWLEDGE
BY AUTHORITY OF THE GENERAL SYNOD
OF THE CHURCH OF IRELAND
MCMLIII.

Plate 129. BCP Church of Ireland 1953 t.p.

Under these conditions, the **Prayer Book of 1928** began to come into use.[v]

It was a large volume because the whole of the 1662 Prayer Book was included together with the new forms identified by a black line in the margin. The Table of Proper Psalms includes all Sundays. The Lectionary no longer follows Cranmer's scheme based on the civic year but follows the ecclesiastical year. The Calendar was improved with St Mary Magdalene and the Transfiguration added to the red-letter days as well as sixteen black-letter saints excluded and twenty-seven new ones added, which included great teachers and English saints. The Ornaments Rubric was printed in full but with a general rubric that permitted vestments for Holy Communion qualified by the requirement for any change to be accepted by the 'good will of the people as represented by the Parochial Church Council'.

An *Introduction to* ***Morning and Evening Prayer*** is provided before the actual services, which start with the verses and responses: *O Lord, open thou our lips*. They also conclude with the third Collect, although other prayers may be added. This shorter form is similar to the 1549 Book, which differed only by beginning with the '*Our Father…*'. Prayers and Thanksgivings were increased greatly with forty-five forms in all. Following the lead of the Canadian revision of 1922, many of these prayers were composed by well-known divines of all periods.

The general rubrics for **Holy Communion** commended the 'ancient and laudable custom' of fasting before Communion but left the practice to be determined by 'every man's conscience in the sight of God'. Bread for Communion could be from a loaf of 'the best and purest wheat bread' or a wafer. Proper Prefaces from the alternative

v Cuming, 1969, p. 221.

service could be used in the 1662 version, as could the methods of administration. Frere's observation that the primitive Church regarded the whole of the Eucharistic Prayer as effecting consecration and not any particular words within it fell on deaf ears. As Baxter observed of the bishops in 1661, 'antiquity is nothing to them when it makes against them'.[vi] In the alternative rite, the Prayer of Oblation follows immediately upon the Words of Institution, and as a consequence, the fine Prayer of Thanksgiving is always said after Communion rather than being an option.

The general rubrics for **Baptism** allowed parents to be sponsors and for a deacon to baptise in the absence of a priest. A lay person was allowed to baptise privately in the case of an emergency. The introduction to the **Marriage service** dropped the reference to 'carnal lusts' and 'brute beasts' and the bride was no longer required to 'obey' her husband. He now 'shares' his worldly goods with her instead of endowing her with them.

The **Burial service** is significantly altered in tone though not in shape by the provision of alternatives stressing comfort for the mourners. Permission is given for the universal practice of saying the prayers in church before the Committal. Cremation is provided for, and an order for the Burial of a Child follows.

The Ordinal and Accession service are followed by an Appendix containing Prime, Compline, A Devotion before Communion and prayers for black-letter saints' days.

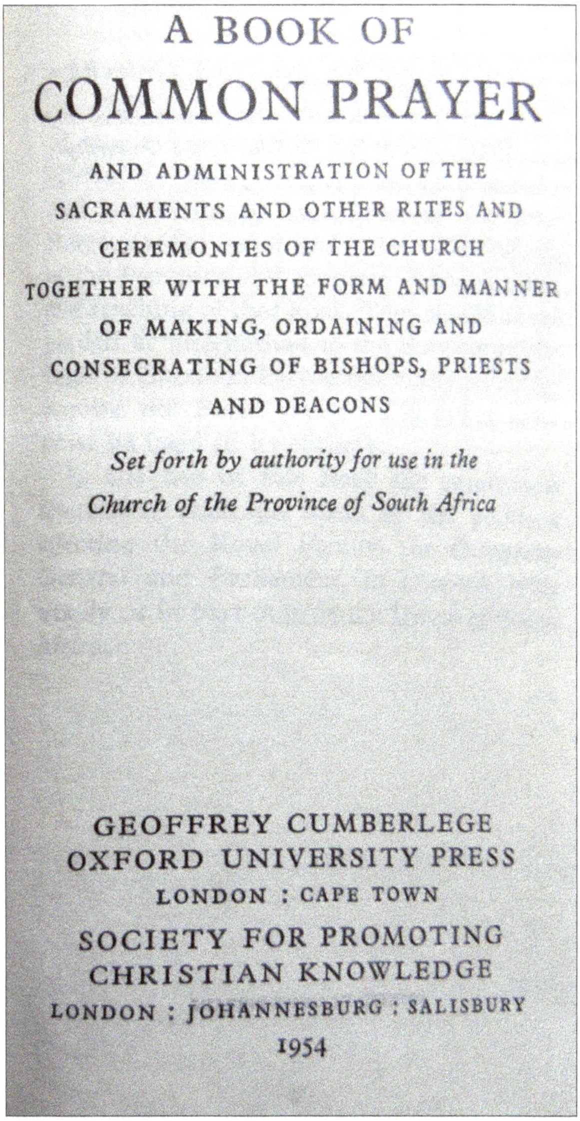
A BOOK OF

COMMON PRAYER

AND ADMINISTRATION OF THE SACRAMENTS AND OTHER RITES AND CEREMONIES OF THE CHURCH TOGETHER WITH THE FORM AND MANNER OF MAKING, ORDAINING AND CONSECRATING OF BISHOPS, PRIESTS AND DEACONS

Set forth by authority for use in the Church of the Province of South Africa

GEOFFREY CUMBERLEGE
OXFORD UNIVERSITY PRESS
LONDON : CAPE TOWN
SOCIETY FOR PROMOTING CHRISTIAN KNOWLEDGE
LONDON : JOHANNESBURG : SALISBURY
1954

Plate 130. Book of Common Prayer Church of South Africa 1954 t.p.

The English Hymnal was published in 1906. Despite expressing a clear Anglo-Catholic position, it was widely and positively accepted due to the high quality of the music edited by

vi Cuming, 1969, p. 231.

Ralph Vaughan Williams. *Songs of Praise* was issued in 1929 but changed many of the words to make them more appealing to liberal sensitivities. *Hymns Ancient and Modern Revised* appeared in 1950 and incorporated many of the favourites from *The English Hymnal* without losing its distinctive flavour.

While parish churches of an Anglo-Catholic persuasion encouraged the practice of daily Eucharistic worship and in small rural country parishes the Prayer Book pattern of 8.00am Holy Communion and 11.00am Matins persisted into the 1960s, there was nevertheless a growing recognition that for most worshippers, one Sunday service would be the norm and that this should be eucharistic. A.G. Herbert's *Liturgy and Society* (1935) gave a new perspective on the Communion service for Anglicans. A celebration of the Eucharist at 9.00, 9.30 or 10.00am with hymns and a sermon combined the purposes of the 8.00am and 11.00am services and restored the Eucharist to its central position in Sunday worship. With the virtual disappearance of Matins, the inclusion of an Old Testament reading and a Psalm were made highly desirable, and the number of communicants necessarily restricted the length of the sermon. The westward-facing position of the celebrant added a visual association with the Last Supper and emphasised that the real celebrant was Christ himself. The eastward-facing position placing the priest among his people together facing an awesome God corresponded well with pre-First World War theological perceptions. The westward position placing God among his people chimed more easily with post-trench-warfare-and-holocaust theology, which required a vulnerable and accessible deity.

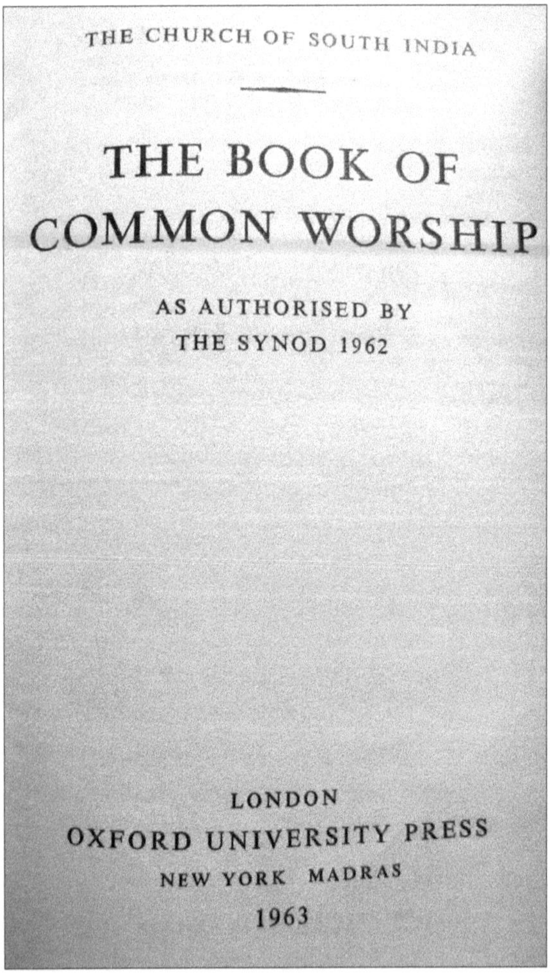
THE CHURCH OF SOUTH INDIA

THE BOOK OF COMMON WORSHIP

AS AUTHORISED BY
THE SYNOD 1962

LONDON
OXFORD UNIVERSITY PRESS
NEW YORK MADRAS
1963

Plate 131. Book of Common Worship of the Church of South India 1963 t.p.

Although the 1928 Book was never passed by Parliament, it was widely used within the Church. It was soon to be overtaken, however, by a climactic event that changed the whole enterprise of Prayer Book revision. This was the publication in 1945 of Dom Gregory Dix's ***The Shape of the Liturgy***, which opened a new era of liturgical studies. Dix argued that Cranmer's 1552 Eucharistic liturgy was simply a memorial and therefore Zwinglian in theology. Dix affirms that the language of the 1549 service did allow a more Catholic interpretation, that Elizabeth favoured a more traditionalist understanding and that Richard Hooker plainly states that Christ is truly present in the Eucharistic elements. Hooker differed from Catholic teaching not because he denied the Real Presence of Christ but because he did not believe this could be clearly defined. It was not possible to say 'how' Christ was present.

Dix argues that:

> ...a great part of Anglican history is taken up with difficulties caused by the fact that the Anglican rite (of 1662) was framed with exquisite skill to express this doctrine (the Zwinglian memorial view) which the Anglican church (as exemplified by the great Hooker) has always repudiated.[vii]

The words of administration of Communion are an example. The 1549 words were replaced by a Zwinglian version in 1552. In 1559, they were stitched together and remained so in 1662 – an Anglican compromise.

Dix demonstrated that primitive liturgies were based on a simple structure implied by Jesus' actions in the New Testament accounts of the Last Supper. In medieval liturgies, including the 1549 revision, the actions of 'taking', 'thanking', 'breaking' and 'sharing' had become obscured and should be clearly demonstrated within the second half of the Eucharistic rite – the Liturgy of the Sacrament. Moreover, he argued that when Jesus said 'Take, eat, this is My Body which is for you. Do this for the *anamnesis* (remembrance) of *Me*' that the 'Me' to which he refers was much more than the Victim of Calvary and implied the whole Christ – past, present and future or pre-existent, incarnate and ascended.[viii]

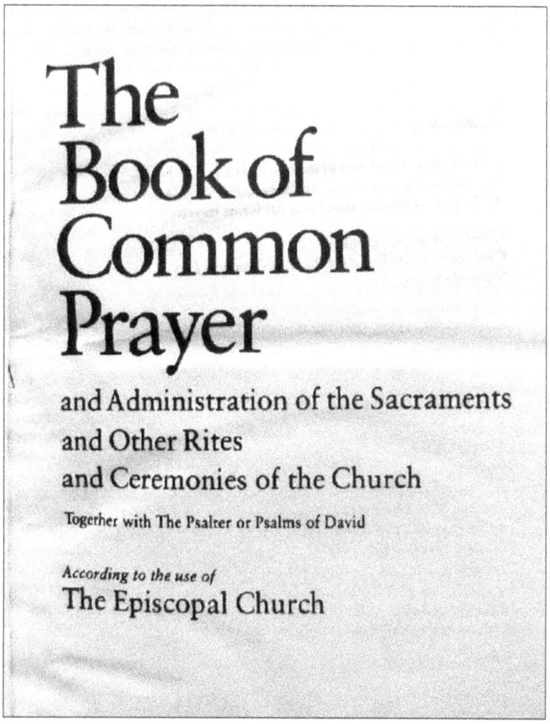

Plate 132. The BCP of the Episcopal Church of the USA 1979.

---

vii Dix, 1945, p. 670.

viii Dix, 1945, p. 670.

Dix's views became highly influential and bore fruit initially in the **Church of South India**, formed after Indian Independence in 1947 by uniting the Protestant and Anglican churches of southern India. Consequently, the new liturgy was influenced not only by the *Book of Common Prayer* but also by the *Book of Common Order* of the Church of Scotland, the *Liturgy of St James* as used in the Syrian churches of Malabar, the Methodist *Book of Offices* and other non-Anglican sources. It is the first ecumenical liturgy based on faithfulness to the Scriptures and intended to be 'an act of the whole people of God in the place where it is used'.[ix]

Plate 133. Advertising the Proposed Book of Common Prayer for the Episcopal Church of India, Pakistan, Burma and Ceylon 1951.

The influence of *The Shape of the Liturgy* upon the **Book of Common Worship of the Church of South India** published in 1963 is to be seen in the introduction of four Scripture readings, in the placing of the Offertory immediately before '*Sursum Corda*', with lay people bringing up the elements, the Eucharistic Prayer as the Great Thanksgiving with the priest facing the people and the separate 'fraction' after the Eucharistic Prayer. The 1662 Prayer of Consecration is kept because of its emphasis on the uniqueness of Christ's sacrifice on the cross, which was especially needed in India in contrast to Hindu sacrificial practice.

A further influence on liturgical debate was the document from the Second Vatican Council, *Constitution on the Sacred Liturgy*. Here, the Roman bishops advocated three alternative Eucharistic Prayers, which encouraged other churches to follow suit. If Rome was not constrained to 'one use', why should Anglicans be?

In 1954, the Church of England appointed a Liturgical Commission to set aside the Reformation debates and explore primitive liturgies. In 1965, the Prayer Book (Alternative and Order Services) Measure received Parliamentary authority and enabled the *Alternative Services: First Series* to be authorised for use by the Synod for seven years from November 1966. This was followed by a second and third series, each of which brought forward additional elements of reform. In 1974, the Church authorised the creation of an *Alternative Service Book*, which, so long as it left the *Book of Common Prayer* untouched, would not need to be brought before

---

ix Cuming, 1969, p. 250.

Parliament. The ASB appeared in 1980 and was permitted initially to have a shelf life of ten years, which was extended to twenty years while the Liturgical Commission produced its final forms of revision.

Of the revisions of the Prayer Book worldwide, that of **South Africa** (1954) was widely regarded as the most satisfactory. Some others include the Church of Ireland (1895 and 1953), Canada (1922 and 1959), America (1928 and 1979) and Scotland (1928). The Church of India, Pakistan, Burma and Ceylon published *A Proposed Prayer Book* in 1951 and a definitive version in 1960. The Archbishops of Africa produced *A Liturgy for Africa* in 1964. The bishops in the Church of South Africa held to the belief that it was the whole Eucharistic Prayer which effected consecration and that the main emphasis of this prayer was of thanksgiving and offering. The sermon was to follow the Gospel, and seasonal sentences and a prayer were provided for the Offertory for the first time in an English Prayer Book. This was widely copied. The South African book appealed to Anglo-Catholics as much as the Irish Book commended itself to Evangelicals.

On 19th October 1928, the General Convention of **the Episcopal Church of the United States of American** approved the third American *Book of Common Prayer* with its own lectionary and other adjustments. The Prayers for use at Sea and the Visitation of Prisoners were discontinued. The new Standard Book was published in 1930. On 2nd February 1976, the Standing Liturgical Commission issued the complete draft of a definitive new *Book of Common Prayer*. It was used from the first Sunday in Advent 1976, as an alternative to the 1928 book. It was made the official Standard Book in 1979, having dropped the word 'Protestant' from its title. It followed the Roman lead of offering multiple versions of the same rite.

A New Zealand Prayer Book was published by The Anglican Church in Aotearoa, New Zealand and Polynesia in 1989. As the subtitle *He karakia Mihinare o Aotearoa* indicates, it draws upon the cultural and spiritual heritage of indigenous people. Many prayers are in the Māori language as well as English.

Plate 134. New Zealand Prayer Book 1989 t.p.

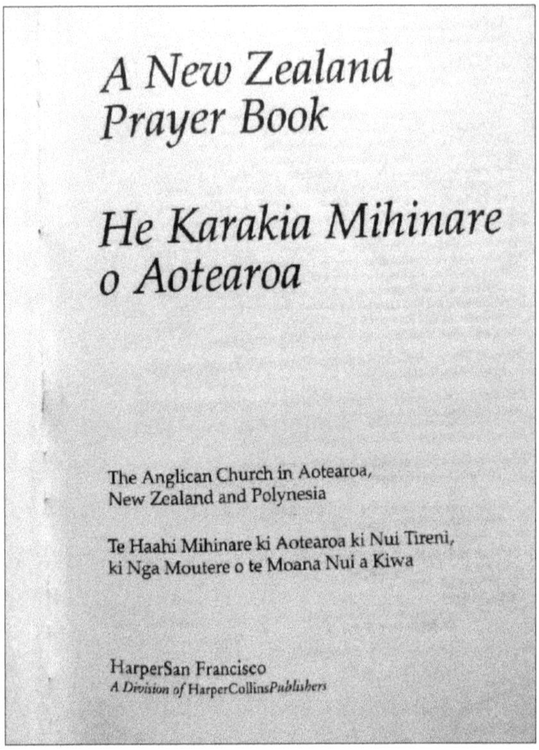

A New Zealand
Prayer Book

He Karakia Mihinare
o Aotearoa

The Anglican Church in Aotearoa,
New Zealand and Polynesia

Te Haahi Mihinare ki Aotearoa ki Nui Tireni,
ki Nga Moutere o te Moana Nui a Kiwa

HarperSan Francisco
A Division of HarperCollinsPublishers

Plate 135. New Zealand Prayer Book 1989 second t.p.

As the Introduction states, 'A Prayer Book for the Church of the Province of New Zealand including...the island nations of the South Pacific...must be a deliberate attempt to allow a multitude of voices to speak.' There is also a strong recognition of the equal place of women and men within the Church and therefore the 'need to choose language which is inclusive in nature and which affirms the place of each gender under God.'

The Alternative Service Book (ASB) proved to be the final single-volume Prayer Book of the English Church, which contained all the services of that Church. One of its innovative features was the Sunday themes offering a two-year cycle of biblical texts around a particular subject. These followed the Church calendar, in which Sundays were designated post Pentecost rather than 'after Trinity' and the Christian year began with the Ninth Sunday before Christmas (also called the Fifth Sunday before Advent) as opposed to Advent Sunday. However, the liturgical colour remained 'green' until it turned to 'violet' on Advent Sunday. The lectionary also provided an 'Introductory Sentence' for each Sunday. These innovative ideas did not last the test of time but that is another story.

The structure of **Morning** and **Evening Prayer** maintained a familiar pattern, but words of introduction were shortened, God is addressed as 'you' throughout the book, and alternative canticles and prayers are provided as well as a 'shorter form' of both services.

Two 'orders' of Holy Communion are permitted: Rite A in modern language and Rite B in more traditional language. Rite A is the result of Dix's scholarship with the four-fold 'shape' clearly identified in the Ministry of the Sacrament (see Appendix 5 for the order together with that of the 1662 Book). Rite A provides for four Eucharistic Prayers, all of which have a clear epiclesis and anamnesis, although the third has a double epiclesis over the people as well as the bread and wine. The order of the 1662 canon is provided in modern language as an option. The number of Proper Prefaces

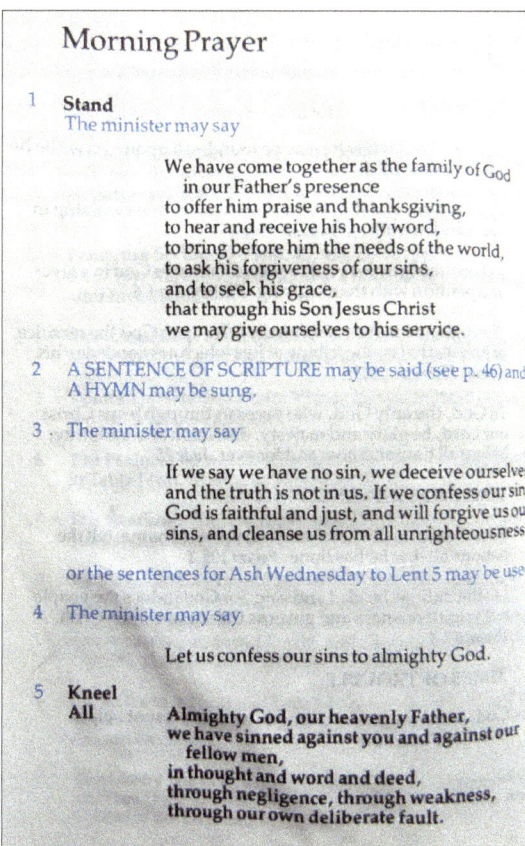

Plate 136. ASB 1980 Morning Prayer. N.B. rubrics in blue.

is greatly expanded, and there are many alternative forms for different parts of the service. New and shorter words of administration are used and preceded by an invitation based on the 1559 words of administration.

Rite B combines elements of the *Book of Common Prayer* order with the new teaching of *The Shape of the Liturgy*. A rubric permits certain elements of the 1662 text – the *Gloria*, Creed, Intercession, Confession, Absolution and Lord's Prayer – to be used instead of the text provided. Two Eucharistic Prayers are printed, the first of which uses the 1662 prayer followed by the Prayer of Oblation and the second incorporating an epiclesis and anamnesis. Three forms of the words of administration are offered, all of which are based on those of the 1549 book. The *Book of Common Prayer*'s Prayer of Thanksgiving is used after Communion.

Initiation Services commence with 'Thanksgiving for the Birth of a Child' and 'Thanksgiving for Adoption'. Baptism and Confirmation come in two forms, with and without Holy Communion as well as forms with Morning and Evening Prayer. These services conclude with 'The Renewal of Baptismal Vows on Various Occasions' and 'Emergency Baptism'. A lay person may perform this final rite, and the rubrics (which are now printed in blue) assure the parents that ultimate salvation and a Christian funeral do not depend on the infant being baptised.

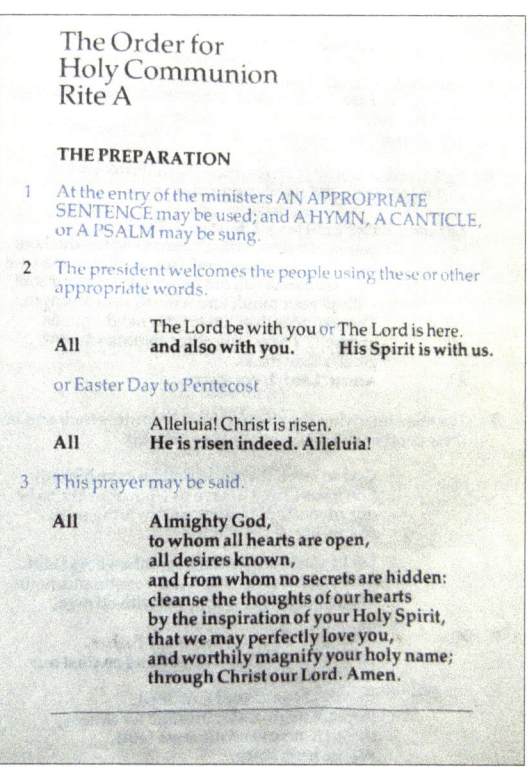

Plate 137. ASB 1980 Holy Communion Rite A.

Optional vows in the **Marriage Service** allow the bridegroom to 'worship' the bride and she to 'obey' him. A form with Holy Communion follows. The Notes for a **Funeral Service** permit considerable flexibility. In the case of a cremation, the Committal may precede the service in church, an option which has become increasingly popular. The rite includes 'Prayers after the Birth of a still-born Child or Death of a newly-born Child' as well as A Form which may be used at the 'Interment of the Ashes and A Service which may be used before a Funeral and…with Holy Communion'.

Sentences, Collects and Readings [for] Lesser Festivals and Holy Days are expanded to include the Unity of the Church, The Peace of the World, In Time of Trouble, At a Marriage, The Sick, The Dying, At a Funeral, A Synod, Those Taking Vows, Social Responsibility, Civic Occasions and others.

The table for Psalms and Readings for Morning and Evening Prayer throughout the year refer to the Revised Standard Version of the Bible. Readings and Psalms for the daily Eucharistic lectionary are derived from the *Ordo Lectionum Missae* of the Roman Catholic Church with adaptations. It is followed by the Table of Sunday Themes. The Liturgical Psalter that concludes the book originated as a separate publication: *The Psalms, a new translation for worship* 1976, by David L Frost and others. With the ASB's life lasting up to the end of the century its publication marks a fitting end to this chapter of the story.

Chapter 10

THE SPIRITUALITY OF THE BOOK OF COMMON PRAYER

A spirituality is the way a person understands their religiously committed life and the way they customarily act in accordance with it. So, for instance, a monk expresses his Christian vocation by taking vows of poverty, chastity and obedience. In what ways does the *Book of Common Prayer* give expression to and encourage the formation of a Christian life?

Writing in the 1960s, Martin Thornton found much similarity between the *Book of Common Prayer* and Bendictine spirituality, believing that 'the adoration of God is the height and end of all life, and the Office is the most perfect praise we can offer because it is the prayer of Christ, through the Church, to the Father.'[i] He found in the Prayer Book an expression of the Trinity itself in so far as the objective offering of praise in the daily Office reflects the transcendence of the Father; that worship in the Holy Eucharist reflects the 'perfect succour offered by God the Son' and that the 'subjective religious element in personal devotion' reflects the Holy Ghost as conceived as indwelling Spirit.[ii] To assess how far this high understanding of Prayer Book spirituality is justified, it will be necessary to give attention to the details of its formation and contents.

The *Book of Common Prayer* did not arise *ex nihilo*. Earlier chapters have already identified the medieval service books used by the Church at the time and how Cranmer adapted them, particularly the *Sarum* use. The invention of printing and the increasing use of the vernacular were contributing factors. Cranmer had contact with Continental reformers and their liturgical works. He was also one of the foremost scholars of his time and was well versed in the patristic writers and sought to incorporate whatever he could of their liturgical understanding. Reform was on the agenda not only of a Protestant kind but in the Catholic Church as well, especially in Spain with the work of Cardinal Quinones. All these factors contributed to the publication of a new Litany and the Order of Communion in 1548. While Henry VIII was on the throne, reform was modest. With the accession of Edward VI as a young king under the influence of his Protestant-leaning uncle, reform gathered pace.

---

i Thornton, 1963, p. 268.

ii Thornton, 1963, p. 274.

These were the influences behind Cranmer's first publication, the Prayer Book of 1549. Some clues to its character lie in the title: THE BOOKE OF THE COMMON PRAYAER AND ADMINISTRATION OF THE SACRAMENTS, AND OTHER RITES AND CEREMONIES OF THE CHURCHE AFTER THE USE OF THE CHURCHE OF ENGLAND. The definite article – 'The' – indicates that this was not to be one book among many, as the Church had been used to before. Here was one service book for all occasions and for everyone's use. This was as much a national and therefore political statement as a religious one. It was a book to bind the nation together under the new leadership of the king as opposed to the pope, for, as the Preface states: 'now from henceforth, all the whole realm shall have but one use'.

Another key word is 'common'. This word has two significant connotations. For Cranmer and subsequent generations, it referred to the shared use of this book throughout the whole realm. It was also intended for ordinary people, at least the literate, and for the non-literate who could hear it read in the churches together with the Great Bible. The intention, as Cranmer wrote in the Preface, was 'that the people (by daily hearing of holy scripture read in the church) should continually profit more and more in the knowledge of God, and be the more inflamed with the love of his true religion.'[iii]

One of Cranmer's greatest achievements, as has already been noted in earlier chapters, was the reduction of the eight medieval offices down to the two of Matins and Evensong. This most significant simplification was made possible by the elimination of ceremonial, of the observation of all but the most important of saints' days, and of special introits and anthems, all of which had made the use of the Book unduly complicated. Cranmer wished to give priority to the consecutive reading of Scripture and to keep only those ceremonies which were edifying. He appealed to St Paul that 'all things be done among you…in a seemly and due order' while recognising that ceremonies could be altered and changed and that other countries might make different choices 'as they shall think best to the setting forth of God's honour, and glory: and to the reducing of the people to a most perfect and godly living, without error or superstition.'[iv]

The Prayer Book was to be a manual of spirituality for lay people, exemplified by the addition of Collects that focused on their concerns: that God might look upon our infirmities, for rain, for fair weather, in time of death and famine, in time of war, in time of any common plague or sickness.

---

iii Quotations from Rhys (1910).

iv BCP 1549 Of Ceremonies.

The first Prayer Book of King Edward VI was but a stepping stone to the much more reformed second Book. In the first Book, Cranmer had retained the medieval and primitive words of prayer that the Holy Spirit should bless and sanctify the holy gifts of bread and wine and that the priest make the sign of the cross over them as he said these words. The 1549 canon also included a clear anamnesis: 'we…make… the memorial which thy Son hath willed us to make, having in remembrance his blessed passion, mighty resurrection and glorious ascension'. These and other elements were perceived by the Catholic-minded bishops led by Gardiner to allow a traditional understanding of transubstantiation and so were two significant elements that failed to survive the reform. The 1552 Book was the poorer for it. When push came to shove, the reform agenda trumped the appeal of primitive liturgies.

Nevertheless, there were significant gains. 'The Order for the Purification of Women' became 'The Thanks Giving of Women after Child Birth commonly called The Churching of Women'. The curate was to toll a bell 'at a convenient time' before Morning and Evening Prayer 'that such as be disposed may come to hear God's word and to pray with him'. Scripture sentences, an extended introduction and prayers of confession were introduced to the beginning of Morning and Evening Prayer.

While modest adjustments were made in 1559, in particular the inclusion of the 1549 words of administration with those of 1552, and in 1662, especially the General Thanksgiving written by Bishop Reynolds, the Prayer Book remained much as it was in 1552. The nationalistic element was reinforced with the inclusion of the **State Services**. In a 1763 edition of the *Book of Common Prayer*, 5th November is commemorated not only for the 'happy deliverance of King James I, and the Three Estates of England, from the most traitorous and bloody intended massacre by gunpowder' but also 'the happy arrival of His Majesty King William' and 'for the Deliverance of our Church and Nation'. To this was added 'A form of Prayer and Fasting to be used yearly on the Thirtieth of January' commemorating the martyrdom of the 'blessed King Charles I'; and on 29th May for thanksgiving for an 'end to the great Rebellion, by the Restitution of the King and Royal Family, and the Restoration of the Government'. To these were added a fourth service of prayer and thanksgiving for the accession of the reigning monarch, which in 1763 fell on 25th October.

These days of national commemoration come 'perilously close to mere nationalism' while giving the Prayer Book an 'unequivocally English identity'. Yet the Prayer Book does reflect the needs of the entire nation seen as coterminous with those of the Church and in that way closer to such texts as Leviticus 19 and the Sermon on the Mount by 'integrating sacred and secular, individual and corporate, the ethical and spiritual'. This is not surprising in an age when 'almost everyone conceived the secular order as divinely ordained'.[v]

One of the most memorable aspects of the *Book of Common Prayer* is its **language**. No longer were people to be taught their faith through the colourful wall paintings of their churches but through the spoken word. The word replacing image and ritual became all powerful. Yet those words themselves derived their impact precisely through the use of images especially those of the Bible: 'we have erred and strayed from thy ways like lost sheep' says the new prayer of confession at the opening of the 1552 service of Morning Prayer. That prayer also reflects the biblical understanding of the heart as the seat of intention and action: 'we have followed too much the devises and desires of our own hearts'. Moreover, it recalls Paul's teaching in Romans 7, 'we have left undone those things which we ought to have done and we have done those things which we ought not to have done'. By eliminating hagiographical stories of the saints, including more psalmody and, in time, printing the whole Psalter, the Prayer Book projects a strongly biblical faith.

Cranmer was writing at an optimal time for the English language, roughly fifty years before Shakespeare, when the language was blossoming into new birth. His fine sense of rhythm was well expressed in the opening verses and responses of Morning Prayer with its three-fold pulse: 'O, *Lord* open *thou* our *lips*', 'And our *mouths* shall show *forth* thy *praise.*'[vi]

Typical of Cranmer's rhetorical style was his use of doubles for emphasis: 'erred and strayed', 'declare and pronounce', 'absolution and remission', 'pardoneth and absolveth', which were his own creation and others he translated from the Latin, 'sins and wickedness', 'let and hindered', 'supplications and prayers', 'church and household', 'power and might'.[vii]

Even more memorable are his **Collects**, which are perhaps the one element of his writing most closely associated with him. He did not invent the form, as many existed in the Latin rites, but he gave them a distinctive flavour of his own while writing many more. The final Collect of Evensong has been identified by several writers as a good example of clarity of form and structure: 'Lighten our darkness, we beseech thee, O Lord, and by thy great mercy, defend us from all perils and dangers of this night, for the sake of thy only Son, our Saviour Jesus Christ.' A Collect of both beauty of structure and doctrinal balance is that of the second Sunday after Easter:

---

v   Mursell, 2001, p. 311.
vi Mursell, 2001, p. 464, note 181.
vii Mursell, 2001, p. 312.

> Almighty God, who hast given thy only Son to be unto us both a sacrifice for sin, and also an ensample of Godly life: give us grace that we may always most thankfully receive his inestimable benefits, and also daily endeavour ourselves to follow the blessed steps of his most holy life; through the same Jesus Christ our Lord. Amen.[viii]

Here we have the typical structure of a salutation to God followed by a statement of divine truth in which the objective grace of Christ's sacrifice is given priority over his example of holy living. This first half is then succeeded by the second, consisting of a petition that we may give thanks (always a priority for prayer) and only then a request that we ourselves might follow his example. Grace precedes response. The prayer concludes with an acknowledgement, as all prayer should, that it is made 'through' Jesus Christ.

As in the book of Genesis, for Cranmer the Word precedes everything else. The essence of all true prayer consists both in our attentiveness to that Word and in God's willingness to hear our response. In his eucharistic prayer of consecration, Cranmer makes this explicit in a beautifully crafted sentence in which the long-delayed principal verb finally crowns both the prayer itself and the entire theology which underlies it:'[ix]

> Almighty God our heavenly Father, who of thy tender mercy didst give thine only son Jesus Christ to suffer death upon the cross for our redemption; who made there (by his one oblation, of himself once offered) a full, perfect, and sufficient sacrifice, and in his holy Gospel commanded us to continue a perpetual memory of that his precious death, until his coming again; Hear us…

While the sixteenth century was a prime time for the memorable construction of the English language from which Cranmer benefitted, his age was not so well served in some aspects of theology, and Cranmer could not help but be a child of his times. A high mortality rate in childbirth and a strong belief in original sin made the birth of a child an anxious time: 'Dearly beloved, for as much as all men be conceived and born in sin…' In the service for The **Visitation of the Sick** and in other places throughout the Book, there is a presumption that suffering, sickness and sin are causally linked and that sickness is a 'visitation' from God. This cannot be criticised as unbiblical, as it was a popularly held belief in Old Testament times, though critiqued in the Book of Job. It was clearly denied by Jesus in the Gospel (see Luke 13:1-5; John 9) although Jesus recognised the unity of the person and accepted that sinful behaviour could lead to physical ill health as implied by his words to the man whom he healed at the Pool of Siloam: 'see you are well! Sin no more, that nothing worse may happen to you' (John 5:14). While the opening Collect prays for the comfort

---

viii Quotations from the Book of Common Prayer are from the 1928 edition.

ix Mursell, 2001, p. 312.

and confidence of the sick person, it is quickly followed by a reminder of the need to repent before it is too late. There was now 'no prayers to the saints, no anointing with oil, no rite of extreme unction, none of the liturgical spectacle that had accompanied generations of Christians through their last moments; rather, just a simple request'[x] for an expression of trust in God.

In contrast, the rite for **'The Form of Solemnization of Matrimony'** is more joyful and is the least changed from its medieval original of all the Prayer Book services. 'Solemnization' may not sound very joyful, but it shows that marriage is a religious rite and not just a civil contract. The prologue recalls the joyful scene of Jesus turning water into the wine of the new kingdom at the marriage at Cana. It has already been noted that Cranmer added to the purposes of marriage that it should be for the mutual 'society, help and comfort that the one ought to have of the other both in prosperity and adversity' possibly from the experience of his own married life. Moreover, to the existing form of the promises, Cranmer added the words 'to love and to cherish'.

Plate 138. Two Victorian BCPs beside the 1662 edition. (a) 'The Finger Prayer Book' carried in the waist-coat pocket of Humphrey Paine's maternal grandfather and (b) a silver bound edition with complete A and M hymns.

---

x Jacobs, 2013, p. 36.

While '**The Order for the Burial of the Dead**' focuses upon those left behind and the soul of the departed is no longer commended to God, though it is assumed that God is pleased to receive it, the rite itself begins and ends with a note of hope. The opening sentence from John 11 affirms that those who believe in Jesus 'will not die for ever'. The service ends with a Collect which looks forward in hope to 'the general resurrection in the last day'. At the centre of the rite, as earth is scattered on the coffin, the curate prays that the body may be changed to 'be like unto [Christ's] glorious body' an important affirmation in a world where life was often short and prone to war and where plague and sickness were not only common but incurable. The rite focuses on the Resurrection of Jesus Christ 'as the pledge and guarantee of the resurrection and glorification of all believers'.[xi]

Jacobs (2013) observes that the Prayer Book treats time in three aspects. The Kalendar walks the reader through the Bible traversing the story of salvation history during the course of the Church's liturgical year. The Occasional Offices of Baptism to Burial incorporate the whole human life from conception to its end. The Offices of Morning and Evening Prayer treat 'the diurnal rhythms of each given day...[rendering] temporal experience accessible and meaningful for each Christian participating in the life of Christ's Church. All this is contained in the one book.'[xii]

This chapter began with a question about Martin Thornton's assessment of the *Book of Common Prayer*. The answer given here is that the book is indeed both beautiful in language and biblical in theology. It is nevertheless a child of its time in both language and theology. It reflects the spirituality of its age and gives expression to the beliefs of the Reformers. But having said that, it was and is an amazing achievement and provided a source of spiritual strength and prayerful support to generations of English-speaking Christians. The *Book of Common Prayer* was John Wesley's Prayer Book. Nicholas Ferrar led prayers from it for his family community at Little Gidding. As George Herbert tolled the church bell, it was to the Prayer Book Offices that he called his people. Alongside these there were thousands of other known and unknown devout believers who benefitted from it.

[xi] Jacobs, 2013, p. 40.

[xii] Jacobs, 2013, p. 41.

EPILOGUE

The story of the *Book of Common Prayer* effectively concluded with the liturgical revision at the latter half of the twentieth century, which culminated in the publication of the *Common Worship* liturgies in 2000. An interesting question remains: how far would Thomas Cranmer and Humphrey J. Paine, the collector of the Prayer Books, regard *Common Worship* to be a worthy successor to the *Book of Common Prayer*?

This author can give a more definite answer regarding Humphrey Paine, as he knew him well, being his son. Although my father had retired in 1974, six years before the publication of *The Alternative Service Book*, he welcomed its arrival. This was because at his heart he was concerned about communicating the Gospel, and having served in the Second World War as a Naval Chaplain, he recognised that the language of the Prayer Book no longer spoke to people in the way that it had. He had already embraced the New English Bible for the same reason.

Both these gentlemen were concerned that the Church's worship should be 'understanded of the people' and in so far as *Common Worship* seeks to achieve this, they might have approved of it. However, there is much in *Common Worship* that would have perplexed Cranmer. He would surely be amazed at the number and complexity of books that make up the *Common Worship* library. But what might be of still more concern to him is the modular approach to liturgy. Flexibility and variety have been prioritised over depth and memorability.

Past generations, including that of Humphrey Paine, if they were clergy, said the Offices daily and knew them by heart. Cranmer's memorable language penetrated their hearts and minds and nourished their souls. They could go beyond the individual words on the page and contemplate the deep meanings of Scripture. The fast-moving nature of today's culture does not appreciate this approach.

While flexibility and variety have produced great riches, especially regarding seasonal material, they have also resulted in the loss of 'common' prayer. Every parish priest is his/her own liturgist. If all used *Common Worship*, there might be some familiarity of use, but many do not. Indeed, many clergy today regret that *Common Worship* is not more flexible than it is. The age-old tension between text and extemporary worship remains as strong today as it was in Cranmer's time, though bishops are not so strict and therefore there is less formal schism. No longer is there 'but one use' in the whole realm, as every parish produces their own *Common Worship* liturgy tweaked to their own preferences.

Nevertheless, there are certainly great gains in *Common Worship*. The seasonal material is a significant enrichment, as is the great variety of Collects and other prayers from churches in the Anglican Communion around the world. Daily Prayer includes a shorter form – Prayer During the Day – as well as the standard form of Morning and Evening Prayer. There is also a form of Night Prayer (Compline). There is a wide choice of biblical canticles and different forms of intercessions, biddings, responses and other prayers. Every Office in seasonal time opens with a new prayer of thanksgiving with an alternative psalm or canticle and includes a new responsory, which may be used between or after the readings. Evening Prayer during seasonal time also includes the ancient practice of an optional opening hymn.

The lectionary maintains consecutive readings, two from the Old Testament and one each from the Gospels and Epistles every day apart from red-letter saints, that is the Blessed Virgin Mary (the Annunciation and Visitation, and 15th August, though the word 'Assumption' is not used), Apostles and Evangelists, John the Baptist, Mary Magdalene, St Joseph, St George, the Holy Innocents, St Michael and All Angels, and All Saints.

The Holy Communion service arguably was most affected by Reformation controversy and is therefore now the most fully restored. Dix's four-fold pattern is maintained in the *Common Worship* liturgies. The epiclesis – the prayer that the Holy Spirit should play a consecrating role – has been restored in all the prayers of consecration. The anamnesis is also present in some form in all but Prayer D. A particularly complete example is that of Prayer F:

> Therefore we proclaim the death that he suffered on the cross,
> we celebrate his resurrection, his bursting from the tomb,
> we rejoice that he reigns at your right hand on high
> and we long for his coming in glory.[i]

However, although we may 'proclaim', 'celebrate', 'rejoice' and 'long', the prayer does fail to say that we do this 'in remembrance' (anamnesis) of Christ, which is more clearly stated in other forms. There is no satisfactory word to translate 'anamnesis'. When Jesus said, 'Do this in remembrance of me,' he did not mean that we should simply think back to the Last Supper or his death on the Cross. What it means is that we are recalling into the present the whole Christ – the crucified, risen and

---

[i] *Common Worship*: copyright © The Archbishop's Council 2000.

glorified Christ. There is, as it were, a telescoping of time so that as we celebrate with the angels and archangels both the past and future are present.[ii]

> The eucharist is not a re-enactment of the Last Supper; it is a fellowship meal with the risen Christ in whom we are one with the Father and have God the Spirit indwelling in our hearts, at which we look back with gratitude to the sacrifice which made this blessedness possible, and which gives us assurance of the greater blessedness to come. Only because of the resurrection are we in this situation; and so a eucharist which does not have post-resurrection existence as its axis is not a proper eucharist at all.[iii]

One of the elements which reflect ancient liturgies features in the third eucharistic prayer from *The Alternative Service Book*. This prayer found favour with eucharistic worshippers and so the *Common Worship* writers included it as Prayer B. Its wording reflects the Non-Juror's book of 1718, which itself emulated Orthodox ancient liturgies. Consider the following phrases:

The Liturgy of St Chrysostom: *'Holy art thou and All-Holy, Thou and Thine only-begotten Son and Thy Holy Spirit. Holy art Thou and All-Holy and sublime is Thy Glory...'*[iv]

The Non-Juror's liturgy of 1718: *'Holiness is thy nature and thy gift, O Eternal King; Holy is thine only begotten Son our Lord Jesus Christ, by whom thou hast made the worlds; Holy is thine Ever-blessed Spirit, who searcheth all things, even the depth of thine infinite perfection. Holy art thou, almighty and merciful God...*

Common Worship Prayer B: *Lord you are holy indeed, the source of all holiness: grant that by the power of your Holy Spirit, and according to your holy will...*[v]

Now that there is no fear of misunderstanding of a transubstantiation interpretation, the Trinitarian nature of the ancient liturgies can enrich our own. Indeed, in this eucharistic Prayer B, there is a double epiclesis with a prayer that the Holy Spirit be poured out upon the gathered congregation as well as on the bread and wine.

The intention of the modern liturgies from *The Alternative Service Book* onwards is that the whole eucharistic prayer is consecratory while recognising that there

---

ii Further exploration of these points may be found in Halliburton R. J. (1974) 'The Peace and the Taking', in Jasper, R.C.D. (ed.) *The Canon of Series 3 in The Eucharist Today: studies on series.* 3rd edn. London: SPCK, pp. 110–116; and Ffrench-Beytagh, G. (1975) *Encountering Light.* London: Fontana Press, pp. 58–60.

iii Baker, 1972, p. 56.

iv *The Divine Liturgy of Saint John Chrysostom*, 1951, p 39.

v *Common Worship*: copyright © The Archbishop's Council 2000.

are highlights included in it. A visible way to make this apparent is to elevate the elements at the conclusion of the prayer, but this is not always followed in current practice.

Not only are the *Common Worship* liturgies rich in their inclusion of some of the elements lost at the Reformation but there is also excellent new material. This is particularly true of the seasonal prayers, especially the new extended proper prefaces, which may be used in Prayers A, B and E. These reinforce the doctrinal message of the appropriate season. The extended preface for Ordinary Time is a fine example:

> It is truly right and just, our duty and our salvation,
> always and everywhere to give you thanks,
> holy Father, almighty and eternal God.
> From sunrise to sunset this day is holy,
> for Christ has risen from the tomb
> and scattered the darkness of death
> with light that will not fade.
> This day the risen Lord walks with your gathered people,
> unfolds for us your word,
> and makes himself known in the breaking of bread.
> And though the night will overtake the day
> you summon us to live in endless light,
> the never-ceasing sabbath of the Lord.
> And so, with choirs of angels…[vi]

There can be no conclusive answer to the question posed at the start of this chapter. What can be said is that the intention of modern liturgists is much the same as that of Cranmer and the Reformers: to offer worthy prayer and praise to almighty God in a language that the people can understand and to which they can contribute. It is ironic that printed texts encourage more congregational participation than extemporary worship led by a single minister. There is ongoing tension between texts which are so simple that they become banal and those which are too linguistically demanding. *Common Worship* attempts to strike a balance. Texts which bear frequent repetition will necessarily not be simple; they need to be grown into and mulled over. Only time will tell if *Common Worship* becomes as much loved and used as the *Book of Common Prayer* has been over the centuries.

[vi] *Common Worship*: copyright © The Archbishop's Council 2000.

APPENDIX 5

1662 BCP

The Lord's Prayer
Collect for Purity
Ten Commandments
One of two Collects for the King
Collect of the Day
Epistle
Gospel
Nicene Creed
Notices and offertory sentence
Sermon or homily or Exhortation (as set)
The collection
Prayer for the whole estate of Christ's Church (additional Exhortation at the priest's discretion)
Exhortation to regular Communion
Exhortation to come to Communion worthily
Invitation to confession
General confession
Absolution
Comfortable Words
Sursum Corda
Proper Preface
'Therefore with angels...'
Prayer of Humble Access
Prayer of Consecration (without epiclesis)
Priest and people receive Communion: (words of 1549 and 1552 combined)
Lord's Prayer with the people repeating after the priest.
Prayer of Oblation; 'mercifully to accept this our sacrifice of praise and thanksgiving...' OR
Prayer of Thanksgiving
Gloria
Blessing by priest or bishop.

ASB 1980 Rite A

THE PREPARATION
A Sentence, Hymn or Psalm may be used/sung
Greeting
Collect for Purity
PRAYERS OF PENITENCE (or after the Intercession)
Summary of the Law
Invitation to Confession (or other suitable words e.g. Comfortable Words)
Confession and Absolution
Kyrie Eleison (optional)
Gloria in Excelsis (optional)
The Collect

THE MINISTRY OF THE WORD
Old Testament Reading (either one or two readings before the Gospel)
Psalm (optional, here or after the NT reading))
New Testament Reading
The Gospel
The Sermon
The Nicene Creed (on Sundays, other forms on other days)
The Intercession (this or another form may be used)
Prayer of Humble Access

THE MINISTRY OF THE SACRAMENT
The Peace (one of two sentences or other suitable words)
THE PREPARATION OF THE GIFTS
Offerings are presented with Scriptural sentence
The Taking of the Bread and Cup (without words) and the Giving of Thanks
THE EUCHARISTIC PRAYER (four options: short seasonal proper prefaces)
THE COMMUNION
The Lord's Prayer
The Breaking of the Bread (with sentence and response)
Agnus Dei (optional here or during Communion)
Invitation to receive Communion (1559 words of administration)
Receiving Communion (new, much shorter words)

AFTER COMMUNION
Post Communion Prayer(s) (either or both may be used)
The Peace (seasonal options)
The Dismissal

ASB 1980 Rite A	COMMON WORSHIP 2000 Order One
THE PREPARATION	THE GATHERING
A Sentence, Hymn or Psalm may be used/sung	**The Greeting**
Greeting	**Prayer pf Preparation** (Collect for Purity)
Collect for Purity	**Prayers of Penitence**
PRAYERS OF PENITENCE (or after the Intercession)	Summary of the Law (or Beatitudes/Comfortable Words/Commandments)
Summary of the Law	Invitation to Confession (seasonal options)
Invitation to Confession (or other suitable words e.g. Comfortable Words)	Confession (or Kyrie eleison with suitable sentences)
Confession and Absolution	Absolution
Kyrie Eleison (optional)	**Gloria in Excelsis** (optional)
Gloria in Excelsis (optional)	**The Collect**
The Collect	THE LITURGY OF THE WORD
THE MINISTRY OF THE WORD	**Readings** (one or two readings from the O.T. and/or Epistles)
Old Testament Reading (either one or two readings before the Gospel)	**Gospel Reading** (seasonal introductory sentence – optional)
Psalm (optional, here or after the NT reading))	**Sermon**
New Testament Reading	**The** [Nicene] **Creed** (or Apostles' Creed or an authorised Affirmation of Faith)
The Gospel	**Prayers of Intercession** (those on pp. 281-289 or other suitable words)
The Sermon	THE LITURGY OF THE SACRAMENT
The Nicene Creed (on Sundays, other forms on other days)	**The Peace**
The Intercession (this or another form may be used)	**Preparation of the Table**
Prayer of Humble Access	**Taking of the Bread and Wine** (gifts are presented, the table is prepared, one or more prayers may be used, the president takes the bread and wine)
THE MINISTRY OF THE SACRAMENT	**The Eucharistic Prayer** (eight options with optional extended seasonal prefaces)
The Peace (one of two sentences or other suitable words)	**The Lord's Prayer**
THE PREPARATION OF THE GIFTS	**Breaking of the Bread** (sentence and response)
Offerings are presented with Scriptural sentence	Agnus Dei (optional)
The Taking of the Bread and Cup (without words) and the Giving of Thanks	**Giving of Communion**
THE EUCHARISTIC PRAYER (four options: short seasonal proper prefaces)	(The president says one of three forms which include the 1559 words of administration)
THE COMMUNION	The Prayer of Humble Access (two forms, one newly written)
The Lord's Prayer	The Communion (one of five authorised words of distribution though none in the text of the service)
The Breaking of the Bread (with sentence and response)	**Prayer after Communion** (one of two options or another suitable prayer)
Agnus Dei (optional here or during Communion)	THE DISMISSAL
Invitation to receive Communion (1559 words of administration)	The Peace (seasonal options)
Receiving Communion (new, much shorter words)	**Dismissal sentence and respons**
AFTER COMMUNION	
Post Communion Prayer(s) (either or both may be used)	
The Peace (seasonal options)	
The Dismissal	

GLOSSARY[i]

ACCESSION SERVICE: A public service to give thanks on the anniversary of a sovereign's accession. It began under king James II in 1685. It has been regularly observed since the accession of Queen Anne. The style was revised by King Edward VII in 1901.

ACT OF UNIFORMITY, or more properly AN ACT FOR THE UNIFORMITY OF PUBLIC WORSHIP. Several Acts of Parliament have regulated the worship of the Church of England beginning with the Act of 1549 (which was never printed in the Prayer Book). However, every edition of the 1552 book included the Act of that year, just as the text of the 1559 Act appeared in each unabridged Prayer Book of Queen Elizabeth I. In 1662 there was a further Act of Uniformity, which appeared after the 1559 Act in all subsequent large-format editions of the *Book of Common Prayer*.

ANAMNESIS: The word which is used in the narrative of the Eucharist in the New Testament (1 Cor 11:24; Lk 22:19). In the context of the Holy Communion service it refers to that part of the Eucharistic (or consecration) Prayer which commemorates the Passion, Resurrection, Ascension and second coming of Christ.

ATHANASIAN CREED or *Quicunque Vult* (its opening words) has appeared in the *Book of Common Prayer* since 1549. In 1662 it came under the heading of AT MORNING PRAYER. It is a confession of faith widely used in Western Christendom. It differs from the Apostles' and Nicene Creeds in form and is not a recognised standard of faith in the East.

AT THE HEALING: A brief service at which English sovereigns used to lay hands on sufferers from scrofula, commonly known as 'The King's Evil'. Although its origins dated back to Norman times, it appeared in print in the *Book of Common Prayer* only on a few occasions between 1706 and 1732.

BLACK RUBRIC: The nineteenth-century unofficial name given to *Declaration on kneeling*, the final rubric at Holy Communion, when the Oxford University Press published the first modern Anglican *Book of Common Prayer* to have rubrics in red (1826/11). By order of the Privy Council and at the insistence of the Scottish reformer John Knox, the 'rubric' had been incorporated in the 1552 *Book of Common Prayer*. It was omitted in 1559 and 1603-4. A modified version was added to the text of 1662.

---

i For further information about the items in this glossary please refer to: Griffiths, 2002; Cross, 1966.

BOOK OF HOURS or HORAE was a pre-Reformation lay person's Prayer Book generally in Latin comprising in the main part the canonical hours of the Breviary (priest's Prayer Book). In the Western Church, the eight commonly recognised Hours are: Matins and Lauds (often used as a single hour), Prime, Terce, Sext, None, Vespers and Compline. Other devotions were commonly included.

CANON OF THE MASS: Although over the centuries there has been much variation concerning which prayers are included under this title it is now generally recognised to comprise those prayers between the *Sursum Corda* ('Lift up your hearts') and the Lord's Prayer. In our present liturgies this is what we call the Eucharistic Prayer. In general terms 'canon' meant 'rule' and this was the unchanging part of the Holy Communion service whereas other elements differed according to the season.

DAILY OFFICES: These comprise Matins and Evensong or Morning and Evening Prayer considered originally as daily services for church members and obligatory services for the clergy.

EPICLESIS refers to that part of the Eucharistic Prayer which invokes the Father to send the Holy Spirit upon the bread and wine to change them into the Body and Blood of Christ.

EUCHARISTIC LECTIONS: The proper Collects, Epistles and Gospels appointed for use at Holy Communion on Sundays and other holy days, commonly called 'propers'.

FOLIO: The term has three meanings: the size of a book, the size of a single sheet of paper, or a single sheet of paper printed with two pages of text on both sides and folded once to form a book of four pages. The first meaning is used here. The size of a folio book is 12" (305mm) x 19" (483mm). Four pages of text printed on both sides and folded twice forms a **QUARTO** book – $9^{1/2}$" (242mm) x 12" (305mm). Double the number of pages and folds forms an **OCTAVO** book – 6" (153mm) x 9" (228mm).

KALENDER: A list of dates for each of the twelve months showing day by day the designated lessons for worship at the daily offices of matins and evensong. Saints' days and holy days are also noted. The spelling was changed to KALENDAR in 1662 and to CALENDAR in 1751.

MATINS AND EVENSONG: The original official names for the DAILY OFFICES to the *Book of Common Prayer* of 1549, changed in 1552 to Morning and Evening Prayer but restored in the headings of the calendar tables from 1662.

METRICAL PSALTERS were frequently bound up with the *Book of Common Prayer* although not part of the official text. The 'Old Version' by Sternhold and Hopkins was used between 1549 and 1696, when a 'New Version' by Tate and Brady took its place until the mid-nineteenth century. However, the dates of the 'old' one finishing and the 'new' beginning overlap and some editions of the *Book of Common Prayer* printed both versions.

OCCASIONAL OFFICES: The section of the *Book of Common Prayer*'s Holy Communion and the Psalter including all the pastoral offices intended for individual Christians as distinct from corporal services for the whole congregation: Baptism, Confirmation, Marriage, Visitation of the Sick, Burial of the Dead, the Churching of Women (or the thanksgiving of women after child-birth).

ORDINAL: *The form and manner of making, ordaining, and consecrating bishops, priests and deacons,* first issued in 1549 and formally incorporated into the *Book of Common Prayer* in 1662.

PLACEBO: (Lat. 'I will please') A traditional title for the Vespers of the Dead.

PRAYERS FOR USE AT SEA: A Cromwellian order of service first included in the *Book of Common Prayer* of 1662, when it immediately followed the Psalter.

PRIVILEGED PRESSES: The copyright of both the Authorised Version of the Bible and the *Book of Common Prayer* vests in the Crown and was for many years licensed to three 'privileged presses', the King's (or Queen's) Printers, and the Universities of Oxford and Cambridge.

PSALTER: The Psalms of David in prose, pointed and arranged for singing or chanting. The psalms of the *Book of Common Prayer* have always been taken from the 1540 edition of the Great Bible of King Henry VIII.

RUBRICS: In the context of Prayer Books, a rubric has been defined as 'an instruction on procedure during service in church, or on other occasions of ministration by the clergy.' Before the Reformation, printed and manuscript service books inscribed these instructions in red. Although they may not be printed in red now printers use contrasting types to distinguish the spoken words of a service from the instructions to priest and people.

STATE PRAYERS: Formal prayers for the Royal Family printed at the end of Matins and Evensong.

STATE SERVICES: A series of special forms of prayer which appeared after the Ordinal at the end of the *Book of Common Prayer*. They were introduced in 1662 and remained until 1859. They included thanksgiving for deliverance from the Gunpowder Plot and the Great Fire of London, for the birth and succession of Charles II and succeeding monarchs.

TABLE OF KINDRED AND AFFINITY (TKA) : This table usually appears as the final item in modern editions of the *Book of Common Prayer*. It was first published by Archbishop Matthew Parker in 1563 and apparently based on the degrees of intermarriage prohibited in Leviticus XVIII. Its presence in the *Book of Common Prayer* dates back to 1681 but it still has no official sanction.

TRANSUBSTANTIATION: In the theology of the Eucharist, the conversion of the whole substance of the bread and wine into the whole substance of the Body and Blood of Christ, only the accidents (i.e. the appearance of the bread and wine) remaining. This distinction between substance and accidents is based on Aristotelian metaphysics and found its classical formulation in the teaching of St Thomas Aquinas in the thirteenth century.

BIBLIOGRAPHY

PRIMARY SOURCES

Horae (Book of Hours) late 14th c. Flemish.

The Prymer or *Prayer Book Of The Lay People In The Middle Ages in English about 1400 AD* (1891)London: Longmans (copy).

THE PRIMER, *set forth* **by the King's Majestie & his Clergy** (c. 1710) London: Richard Grafton (17.8.1546 facsimile re-print).

Wilson, H.A., MA (ed.) (1908) **THE ORDER OF HOLY COMMUNION 1548**. London: printed for the Henry Bradshaw Society by Harrison and Sons (facsimile of the British Museum copy).

Rhys, E. (ed.) (1910) **First** and **Second Prayer Books of Edward VI** *(Everyman Library)*. London: J.M. Dent and Sons.

The Book of Common Prayer As Issued In The Year 1549, In The Reign Of Edward The Sixth (1896) **Facsimile limited edition**, one of 300 on handmade paper.

The First Book of Common Prayer of Edward VI and The Ordinal of 1549 together with The Order of the Communion, 1548 (1870) London: Oxford and Cambridge, Rivingtons (copy).

The Book of Common Prayer Noted by John Merbecke 1550 (1844) London: William Pickering (facsimile).

Elizabethan **Book of Common Prayer**; missing title page.

The Book of Common Prayer (1615) London: Robert Baker.

The Book of Common Prayer (1623) London: John Bill and Bonham Norton.

The Book of Common Prayer with the **Holy Bible** and **Apocrypha** (1629) London: Bonham Norton and John Bill.

The Book of Common Prayer (1637) 'Laud's Liturgy' for Scotland, Edinburgh: Robert Young.

The Book of Common Prayer (1637) printed 1712 for 1715 uprising.

Black Letter Prayer Book of 1636 (1871) used at the Savoy Conference by Sancroft (facsimile).

The Book of Common Prayer (1661) London: John Bill.

The Book of Common Prayer (1662) Cambridge: John Field.

The Book of Common Prayer (1680) London: John Bill.

The Book of Common Prayer (1683) Oxford: M. Pitt.

The Book of Common Prayer (1685) London: John Bill.

The Book of Common Prayer (1694) Cambridge: John Hayes.

The Book of Common Prayer (1704) London: Charles Bill.

The Book of Common Prayer (1716) Oxford: John Baskett.

The Book of Common Prayer (1717) Oxford: John Baskett (engraved on 189 silver plates by John Sturt).

Le Livre des Prieres Communes (1717) Oxford: J. Baskett (French and English parallel columns; Royal binding).

The Book of Common Prayer (1727) London: John Baskett (Non-Juror's liturgy of 1718).

The Book of Common Prayer (1762) Cambridge: John Baskerville.

The Book of Common Prayer (1787) Cambridge: John Archdeacon.

The Book of Common Prayer according to the use of the **Protestant Episcopal Church of the USA** (1789) London: J. Debrett ('the Proposed Book').

The Book of Common Prayer (1795) Oxford: W. Jackson and W. Dawson.

The Book of Common Prayer (1801) London: John Reeves.

The Book of Common Prayer (1803) Oxford: Dawson, Bensley and Cooke.

The Book of Common Prayer (1815) London: John Reeves.

The Book of Common Prayer (1824) Edinburgh: D. Hunter Blair and J. Bruce.

The Book of Common Prayer (1840) London: John W. Parker, for SPCK with 'Figure of Faith'.

*The Psalter...according to the use of the...***Church of Sarum** (1852) London: John Masters.

The Book of Common Prayer (1853) London: William Pickering.

The Book of Common Prayer according to the use of the **Protestant Episcopal Church of the USA** (1855) London: William Pickering.

The Book of Common Prayer The Finger Prayer Book (after 1871) Oxford: Oxford University Press/London: Henry Frowde.

The Book of Common Prayer according to the use of *The Church of Ireland* (1895) Dublin: Association for Promoting Christian Knowledge.

The Coronation Prayer Book (1902) Oxford: Oxford University Press/London: Henry Frowde.

The Coronation Prayer Book (1911) Oxford: Oxford University Press.

The Book of Common Prayer The Book of 1662 with Permissive Additions and Deviations Approved 1927 (1928) Oxford: John Johnson, Oxford University Press.

The Book of Common Prayer with Additions and Deviations Approved in 1928 (1928) Oxford: Charles Batey, Oxford University Press.

The Scottish Book of Common Prayer (1929) Edinburgh: Cambridge University Press.

The Book of Common Prayer…according to the use of the **Protestant Episcopal Church in the United States of America** (1938) New York: Thomas Nelson.

The Book of Common Order of the **Church of Scotland** (1952) Oxford: Geoffrey Cumberlege, Oxford University Press.

The Book of Common Prayer according to the use of the **Church of Ireland** (1953) Dublin, Belfast, Limerick: A.P.C.K.

The Book of Common Prayer…for use in the **Church of the Province of South Africa** (1954) Oxford: Geoffrey Cumberlege, Oxford University Press.

The Church of South India (1963) *The Book of Common Worship: As Authorised by the Synod 1962*. London, Oxford University Press.

The Book of Common Prayer…According to the use of **The Episcopal Church** (1979) New York: Church Publishing Incorporated.

The Alternative Service Book 1980 (1980) Oxford: A. R. Mowbray, Oxford University Press.

A New Zealand Prayer Book (1997; originally published by William Collins, 1989) San Francisco: Harper Collins.

The Divine Liturgy of Saint John Chrysostom. 7th edn. (1951) Leighton Buzzard: The Faith Press.

SECONDARY SOURCES

Baker, J.A. (1972) 'The "Institution" Narratives and the Christian Eucharist' in Ramsey, I. T. (ed.) *Thinking about the Eucharist: Essays by Members of the Archbishop's Commission on Christian Doctrine*. London: SCM Press, pp. 38–58.

Benton J.H. (1910) *The Book of Common Prayer its Origin and Growth*. Boston: The Merrymount Press.

Campbell, D.A. (1929) *The Scottish Book of Common Prayer*. London: SPCK.

Common Worship (2000) London: Church House Publishing.

Cross F.L. (ed.) (1966) *The Oxford Dictionary of the Christian Church*. Oxford: Oxford University Press.

Cuming J.G. (1969) *A History of Anglican Liturgy*. London: Macmillan and Co.

Dix, Dom Gregory (1964[1945]) *The Shape of the Liturgy*. London: Dacre Press, Adam and Charles Black.

Duffy, E. (2005[1992]) *The Stripping of the Altars*. 2nd edn. New Haven: Yale University.

Griffiths, D.N. (2002) *The Bibliography of the Book of Common Prayer 1549-1999*. London: The British Library.

Harrison, D. (1959) *The Book of Common Prayer*. London: SPCK.

Jacobs, A. (2013) *The Book of Common Prayer: A Biography*. Princeton: Princeton University Press.

Jones, C., Wainwright, G. and Yarnold, E. (eds.) (1978) *The Study of Liturgy*. London: SPCK.

MacCulloch, D. (2009) *A History of Christianity*. London: Penguin Books.

Maltby, J. (1998) *Prayer Book and People in Elizabethan and Early Stuart England*. Cambridge: Cambridge University Press.

Mursell, G. (2001) *English Spirituality*. London: SPCK.

Ratcliffe, E.C. (1949) *The Booke of Common Prayer its Making and Revisions 1549-1661*. London: SPCK.

Spinks, B.D. (2017) *The Rise and Fall of the Incomparable Liturgy*. London: SPCK.

Suter J.W. and Cleveland G.J. (1949) *The American Book of Common Prayer: its Origin and Development*. New York: Oxford University Press.

Thornton, M. (1963) *English Spirituality*. London: SPCK.

ABOUT THE AUTHOR

The Reverend Peter S. Paine was brought up in the same rectory in the Norwich Diocese as his father was born in and lived as incumbent. He attended Kings College London (BD, AKC) and Anglia Ruskin University in Cambridge (MA). He served two curacies in Leeds (St Aidan's) and Harrogate (St Wilfrid's) before his appointment as Vicar of Holy Spirit Beeston Hill in south Leeds where he was married to Carol in 1979. After serving for eight years in the Seacroft Team Ministry in east Leeds, the family of four children moved to Martham in Norfolk where Peter was incumbent of a benefice of four rural parishes for fourteen years. His last post was the benefice of Repton with Foremark and Newton Solney in the Derby diocese. He is now retired and living on the Lancashire coast.

ALSO BY THE AUTHOR:

Crumbs for the Journey: A Short Anthology of Spiritual Reflections
Published 2019, New City Press, London.

For more titles from Beaten Track Publishing,
please visit our website:

https://www.beatentrackpublishing.com

Thanks for reading.